What Others are Saying About
Short Stories for the Long Haul

"Good stories can engage, entertain, and teach useful lessons. Exceptional stories challenge us to think deeply about who we are and how we relate to others, with a few even inspiring us to take action. *Short Stories for the Long Haul* is a collection of short, but exceptional, stories and thought-provoking reflections that will capture your attention, speak to your heart, and give you the insight you need to improve your relationships with the people that matter most in your life."

--Michael Patterson, Ed.D.
Co-author of *Have a Nice Conflict: How to Find Success and Satisfaction in the Most Unlikely Places*

"Any couple, whether their relationship is sound, or is seriously challenged, will benefit from this book. Dr. Shelton combines sound biblical perspectives with deep insights into the often-complex dynamics of marital relationships. Of particular note are the many descriptions of common marital struggles, which are often baffling to the couples. What Dr. Shelton is able to artfully present are how these difficulties arise, what maintains them, and most importantly, how they may be overcome. One of Dr. Shelton's strengths is untangling the complex and describing these in an easily understood very readable manner. I highly recommend this to couples who want to improve their marital relationship."

--Mark Balen, Ph.D. Clinical Psychology, Licensed Marriage, Family, and Child Therapist; 38 years of experience with couples, adolescents, and families.

"Larry's book is a refreshingly new approach to addressing the complicated needs of marriages today. His easy-to-read stories and focused questions are very helpful at getting to the core issues all marriages face. Jesus once said, 'What God has joined together let no man separate.' Jesus was telling us in those words that we can work our marriages out together. But we need God intimately involved in our lives to do it. This book can help you do that and help you experience all God wants to give you in your marriage."

--Pastor Marty Berglund, Senior Pastor; Fellowship Alliance Church, Medford New Jersey

"I was so excited when I learned that Larry was going to write this book because he has tremendous insights into relationships and has been instrumental in helping so many couples grow in their marriage. You will not be disappointed if you dive into the stories and engage in conversation guided by my friend."

-Dr. Bruce Terpstra, District Superintendent of the Metropolitan District of the C&MA, author of *Three Passions of the Soul*.

SHORT STORIES FOR THE LONG HAUL

Short Stories for the Long Haul

a guidebook of hope and greater health for every marriage

Dr. Larry G. Shelton

Consentia Group Publishing

SHORT STORIES FOR THE LONG HAUL

Content adapted with permission related to *Three Passions of the Soul©*, by Dr. Bruce K. Terpstra

Printed in the USA

Cover photo © Hume Lake Christian Camps Inc. Used by permission.

Illustrations by Heather Silva

ISBN: 0692105190

ACKNOWLEDGEMENTS

This book would not be possible were it not for Jesus Christ. I am grateful beyond my ability to express for His unconditional love demonstrated on the Cross and His continued daily expression of love through His gifts of guidance, insight and provision.

One of the greatest gifts He has given me is my wife of 45 years. Faith truly is my Soulmate. She has lived up to her name in good times and bad; faithful through the years. Without her, I wouldn't have much to write and what I might have written would have likely been void of experiential depth. I thank my God daily for such an amazing wife and best friend. This book is dedicated to her.

I am also grateful for the many people who prayed for and assisted in various ways the writing of this book. They include:

-Mary Rush who was willing to give hours of editorial assistance.

-Those who attended the beta versions of the Soul Mates For Life training. Thank you to every one of you who came to those trainings, then gave feedback. Many also attended the beta versions of "Short Stories for the Long Haul". Your eager responsiveness, participation and encouragement were inspirational and invaluable.

-The staff of Neighborhood Church Chico, California. You gave me support, encouragement, prayer, advice. You were and are a God send! Thank you.

CONTENTS

Appendices

INTRODUCTION

You are so wise! How do I know? The ancient historical document known as the book of Proverbs, written by one of the wisest men who ever lived said, "Start with God—the first step in learning is bowing down to God; only fools thumb their noses at such wisdom and learning." I trust you have already "started with God"[1] and are continuing to move forward as He directs you. Only fools, we are told, would walk away from such an opportunity to acquire more wisdom for life in general and for living with one's spouse.

So, why Short Stories for the Long Haul?

Do you want to have an enduring, wonderful marriage? Almost everyone would answer, "yes". Well, in order to have an enduring, wonderful marriage one needs to, "live with your wife (husband) with proper understanding." Proper understanding requires self-awareness and relational awareness. And that requires communicating about everything that involves the two of you. This book provides a brilliant opportunity to have deep conversations that will greatly enhance a progression of mutual awareness, understanding, acceptance, appreciation, and effectiveness. (These conversations can be deepened even more by taking the recommended online assessments[2].)

In addition, it is often stated that the divorce rate amongst people-of-faith is the same as those who are not people-of-faith.

However, according to a University of Connecticut study[3], the divorce rate for those who don't practice any kind of faith is 60% and for those who attend religious services regularly it is 38%. Imagine how the divorce might adjust downward even more for those who: regularly attend church, <u>and</u> receive SoulmatesForLife[4] training, read the Bible together, pray and journal? Seeing as how divorce is the second most traumatic experience in an adult person's life, and the fourth most stressful event in a non-adult's life, it would seem wise for people to do and use all they can to protect themselves against divorce.

All to say, "Be encouraged," and, "Way to go!" By purchasing this book, you have taken a significant first-step towards a deeper relationship with God and deeper relational-awareness of yourself, your spouse and even others."

[1] If you are interested in learning more about becoming a follower of Christ turn to appendix "A" on pages.
[2] For these assessments go to Consentiagroup.com
[3] Bradley R.E. Wright, *Christians are Hate-Filled Hypocrites...and other Lies You've Been Told,* (Minneapolis, MN: Bethany House, 2010), p. 133.
[4] SoulmatesForLife is a registered domain name (SoulmatesForLife.com).

Book Format

Each chapter covers a particular topic applicable to marriage and/or family life. Chapters start with a topical short story, or if you prefer you can call it a "case study." Couples are expected to make the time to read the short story out loud together. Because the short stories are, well, short (some shorter than others), it is assumed the reader will fill in the "blanks" when the story lines take time-saving "jumps". This is intentional not only because it is a short story, but it also may provide couples the opportunity to spend time together "filling in the blanks" as a way to learn more about each other. Be sure to set aside at least 15 minutes for reading the short stories.

The chapters are not arranged in order of intended use. Pick and choose the ones you want to experience in whatever order you determine until you have completed all 12. It's up to you to start with whatever topics are most needed or most interesting to you at any particular point in your marriage journey together.

Also included in this guidebook are the daily devotionals for couples. The daily devotionals follow the short story and are in sync with the topic of the week. My hope is you will use the daily devotionals to increase the times you and your spouse spend in the Word as well as praying and journaling together. May these practices expand the spiritual depth of your relationship with God and each other.

There are a number of couple's and group questions based on the Strength Deployment Inventory®, Strengths Portrait® and/or Overdone Strengths Portrait® (®Registered trademarks of Personal Strengths Publishing, Carlsbad CA). It is strongly recommended that you take advantage of these insightful assessments; they will assist you in realizing greater depths of personal and relational awareness. You can learn more about these online assessments and/or a SoulmatesForLife training event by contacting ConsentiaGroup.com or SoulmatesForLife.com and/or contacting Dr. Larry G. Shelton at **drlarrygsC2L@gmail.com.**

A "SoulmatesForLife" training event will help you unpack your results and greatly enhance your understanding of your Motivational Value System®. (Your motivation is what drives your behavior as a "system" when things are going well, and it becomes a "sequence" when things aren't going well.) SoulmatesForLife training is a very unique workshop which includes education offered by the leader as well as the participants thus creating an exceptional transformational experience. However, the book is designed to be used by couples who have or have not attended SoulmatesForLife and you can simply skip over questions that reference SDI® assessment information.

This book is well suited for individual couples or groups that decide to experience this journey together. If you are wanting to start a small-group, Short Stories for the Long Haul can provide a great study. Here's an example of a small-group weekly schedule:

- Saturday: Couples read the short story for the topic of the week.
- Sunday: Gather together. Group and assessment discussion questions are in Appendix B at the back of this book.

- Monday-Friday: Couples' share devotionals which include a daily "PBJ": Prayer, Bible reading and Journal. (See the end of each chapter.)

Of course, you might want to use a different "days of the week" format. This is merely a suggestion to give you an idea of "how" to apply this to a group.

In conclusion, I Peter chapter 3:7 (NASB) reminds us that husbands (wives too!) are encouraged to live with their wives with "understanding". This book is designed to help you do just that. No matter how good or, how "challenged" your marriage may be, there is always room for greater understanding of each other, right?

So, you are about to experience learning that could very well rock your marriage and family life and the rest of your relationships as well. It is already doing so for others.

Enjoy, fellow traveler!

Dr. Larry G. Shelton

PS: I encourage you to have a Bible or Bible app available whenever you use this guidebook. Looking up related verses and/or versions can be very helpful. All verses are from the New International Version of the Bible unless otherwise noted.

Chapter One
Going Deep

Lori was a beauty consultant and Tom a recent graduate of the fire academy. Her income had its up and downs but with Tom landing a full-time job at the fire department, there was enough financial stability to finally tie the knot. Having lived together for some months prior to their announced engagement, they felt they knew each other pretty well, at least well enough to get married.

They had revealed much about themselves in various carefree, rambling conversations. Consequently, they knew:

- Lori was raised in a reasonably healthy Christian home. Tom was raised in a drug culture home.

- Lori was used to a calm home environment; Tom was used to his parents having drug and/or alcohol induced shouting matches.

- In Lori's home of origin, though they weren't rich there always seemed to be enough money for whatever was needed. Tom grew up in a home where there was never enough food, much less enough money; most income was spent by his parents on drugs.

- Communication under Lori's parent's roof was usually tactful and considerate. In stark contrast, it seemed like the roof would regularly be raised in Tom's home; in-your-face bluntness reigned.

- Lori's parents were tactfully but openly affectionate towards each other; theirs was a genuine, long-term love. Tom's parents loathed more than loved each other. As misguided champions of being authentic and transparent, they were openly combative no matter what the setting or who might be within ear shot.

Obviously, these soon-to-be-newlyweds came from two different worlds. Yet their worlds had sovereignly collided. Now, here they were engaged and ready to commit themselves to each other in the exclusive, affectionate covenant of marriage. With as much wisdom as their respective ages could afford, they resolved to be married for the rest of their earthly existence. Their wide-eyed enthusiasm and near boundless courage was an inspiration to all who knew them. When they were in public social settings, it was common for Tom and Lori's obvious love for each other to inspire others. Their relationship would prompt even wounded cynics and skeptics to dare to wonder if there might still be hope for their own marriages.

Tom and Lori were going to make this marriage work. In fact, they just knew they could make it work having learned so much from their parents' examples. They both had experienced good and bad lessons, so they were certain they knew what to model and what to avoid.

They were so much in love! And about a month before the wedding, in no small part due to Lori's recent recommitment to

Christ and her effective prayers, Tom, with the help of their marriage counselor, surrendered his life to the Savior. What a wonderful new dynamic this added to their relationship. With God's help, they really could fall much deeper in love!

Together their newly discovered spiritual hunger caused them to wonder and hope things like, is it possible to fall even deeper in love with God? Would God truly accept them "warts and all" given their less than perfect premarital histories? Could and would God fall deeper in love with them?

With these questions and all the implied but wonderful Grace-of-God potential responses, it seemed all too easy to reason, "Now that we are a Christian couple, our relationship is going to be nearly perfect; every challenge is going to be easy to resolve." Still, they were wise enough to sign up for more pre-marital counseling with the man who had introduced Tom to Christ. During those sessions, they would soon discover they had numerous unspoken expectations of this marriage and each other.

With each session, they discovered more about those expectations as well as their differences and similarities. The counselor realized they didn't really understand as much about each other as they should prior to getting married. But the invitations had already been sent out, and contracts had been signed; their wedding date was rapidly and inevitably drawing near. So, at the counselor's recommendation, they signed up for a marriage workshop already scheduled for just weeks after their honeymoon.

The wedding went great. The honeymoon was fantastic! And now with just a few weeks of married life under their belts, here they were at this rustic conference center located in the Sierra Nevada mountains. The training the counselor had recommended came in the form of a weekend SoulmatesForLife marriage retreat. And what a weekend it would prove to be!

On Friday night, the first night of their retreat, dinner was superior and the group session that followed was even better. The speaker did an excellent job of communicating and relating his own real-life experiences; he was "on fire". When Friday night's activities were over they headed back to their cottage. They had had an exhausting week. They fell into bed then slept soundly which was uncommon because neither of them usually slept well the first night in an unfamiliar bed. Awakened by the camp bell, they got out of bed and readied themselves for what might lie ahead. They would soon discover that their eight solid hours of continuous sleep would serve to enhance the days' activities; and even the night's.

The first meal of the day was also signaled by the camp bell; it's second ringing of the morning. When they arrived at the dining hall they saw that the assortment of breakfast food was enormous and fantastic! Every young mother attending was especially dazzled by the reality that this day they would not have to prepare food for anyone but themselves. It wasn't that everyone there needed to eat a lot more, but the energy this feast provided would prove to be a requirement for all who desired to go deeper with their spouse this day. The buffet line moved quickly. With selections made and consumed, and their stomachs filled beyond what was customary for a routine day, Tom and Lori transitioned from the dining hall to the camp's main meeting hall where nothing "routine" was about to take place.

As they walked into the meeting hall the first morning, a comedic "ice-breaker" video was already playing on the projection screen. It was truly funny. Almost everyone in the room was now smiling. Announcements, a necessary administrative issue for such gatherings, had to be made; they were short and helpful. Then with a brief but gracious introduction, a worship team was invited to the stage. They plugged in, tuned up, and adjusted their mics as the leader encouraged everyone to make their preparation to worshipfully enter the presence of God. A few moments of prayerful silence were shared as participants adjusted and tuned in their hearts. When the worship team's leader humbly concluded the participant's prayerful silence with an "Amen", the Spirit's prompting caused everyone to understand it was time to give back to God. From the first song, hearts hungry to worship joined in. Every voice took part as familiar heart-felt worship was offered to the King. When less familiar songs were led by the band, those who didn't know the melody could still sense these musical offerings were speaking the language of their souls. Absent was any spirit of division. Truth-filled worship flowed freely. It was healing, encouraging and powerful. As His children gave Him unified praise, one could almost sense the smile on the Father's face.

Always the case, the Provider was not about to let His children out-give Him. So, in addition to His peaceful presence, He gave them a speaker, a man after His own heart. This man was able to speak from the depths of his learning as well as from the pain of his own experience and the experiences of others he had coached and counseled. The content of his message and his illustrations were so insightful and incisive that those listening were inclined to wonder, "How did he know that about me; about us?" His not-long-enough message was over almost before it seemed to begin. Through the speaker's concluding remarks, couples were encouraged to further discuss what his message had covered. They were compelled to seize the moment through spending time together in some outdoor place of their choosing.

With a closing song and prayer, the session was over. Of course, lunch time was also announced. But no one wanted to leave due to the peaceful (healing?) presence of the Spirit. Even though the morning's group session time was over, the couple's sharing time wasn't. Willing couples knew there was more truth and deeper relationship to be gleaned. So, eventually everyone filed out; some to find their "secret place" where they would talk further about the morning's topic. Tom and Lori already knew where they would go. During their first evening's brief exploration of the camp, they had discovered a nearby picnic table situated close to the lake's edge. They already knew they would go back to that peaceful spot. It had such a beautiful vista of most of the lake with the mountains of King's Canyon providing a majestic background. It was the perfect place to discuss the retreat speaker's message and the truths that spoke most personally to each of them.

At the lake side, they responded well to the speaker's challenge. Painful as well as pleasant experiences were shared. It was both frightening and freeing at the same time. Prompted by the absence of any hint of rejection, and from the depths of their souls, they began to reveal more of their past histories.

Sooner than expected, the camp bell rang out indicating lunch time. "Wow, lunchtime sure came quickly today!" They smiled when they both said that sentence at the same time. Their smiles communicated mutual admiration and appreciation for the revealing risks taken and the loving acceptance both had just experienced. Tom and Lori reluctantly yet happily gathered their belongings then walked hand-in-hand to the dining hall. The meal was good.

When lunch was over, the camp host announced they were free until dinner; free to enjoy time alone or with other couples. And any activity the camp offered was theirs, no charge. All they had to do was signup. Instead of hurrying through the afternoon, Tom and Lori chose less activity over more. They just needed some "us" time. Together they pondered, "What carefree activity shall we choose first?"

Again, hand-in-hand, they decided to stroll around the lake. After they had walked a few hundred yards, another couple, Tim and Stacy, caught up with them and for a while walked alongside them. From their conversation, Tom and Lori realized Tim and Stacy had been married longer and they had children. Tim and Stacy shared with Tom and Lori how nice it was to be able to hold hands without the responsibility of also holding the hands of their children. They dearly loved their children but such carefree timelessness was rare for Tim and Stacy these days. Their discussion couldn't help but make Tom and Lori wonder if they would always make time for each other. Tim and Stacy were on a faster pace around the lake so they offered their "see ya laters" and moved ahead.

When Tom and Lori finally rounded the last corner of the lake trail, the camp's boat dock was in sight. Before the lake walk was even completed, canoeing was already calling. The lake's beautiful azure-blue waters were irresistible. They walked up to the dock's office, quickly signed a release form, donned some life jackets and grabbed a couple of well-worn but still useful paddles. They had canoed before so there was little risk of falling in. As they pushed away from the dock they re-experienced the joy of silently gliding on the water.

Sometimes they paddled. Sometimes they simply drifted being moved along by the moderate winds that intermittently wafted the water's surface. It was so peaceful. It restored their souls. Alone on the water they were trying to "go deep" again, but it just wasn't working. The problem was this: both of them were facing forward and they were so many feet apart. Also, knowing that sound travels great distances over water, they had a very real concern that others would hear their secret conversations. They didn't really care to have anyone else "in" on their disclosures. So, they decided to head back to the dock and then to their "secret place"; to their lake side picnic table in the pines.

Now uninhibited and settled in at the table, still motivated by the retreat speaker's challenge, they began to reveal things from the depths of their souls. As each recalled their growing-up years, they learned of the unintentional lies they were sure they had heard from their imperfect parents, siblings and peers. She told him how as a teenager she had entertained a lot of harmful introspection which in turn, deposited in her soul, a significant cache of seriously dark thoughts. It helped him remember his own. As rebirthed beings they shared their growing awareness of the spiritual battles the retreat speaker had referenced. It caused them to wonder, "Did those dark thoughts typical of their adolescent years originate exclusively from their own souls? Or what unearthly, ill-intentioned beings might be capable of instigating such evil ideas?"

Still at the picnic table, their ongoing conversation revealed that growing up, Lori had many close friends including her mother who was a trusted confidant. Tom on the other hand had never had a close friend much less a confidant. Talking to himself even while Lori was talking to him, Tom couldn't help but wonder, "Can I truly be this vulnerable with this beautiful woman? Have I really found someone I can talk to about…anything? Have I finally found my first faithful friend? Will she love me my entire life? Will I find complete acceptance and security with her? Will she provide the significance my soul has craved as far back as I can remember?" Their times at the lakeside picnic table were rich and deep; hours passed quickly. As it turned out, this session too would be brought to a close when the camp's large bell rang out from its wood-beamed open tower. This time its tolling indicated dinner and that the activities of the second evening were about to begin. Tom and Lori were ready for more!

As they stood in line they could see and smell that the opulent dinner buffet would not disappoint anyone. The choices were numerous. The food and fellowship around the tables were excellent. Meal time came and went quickly, again. The camp host encouraged them to move to the meeting hall as soon as possible. There, a meal for their souls had been prepared. His claim would prove to be quite accurate both for the group session and for what he couldn't have imagined for Tom and Lori.

True enough, the evening session was awesome. The worship was empowering and the speaker inspiring. The session concluded at nine and for many of the participants it would be the conclusion of their day. But not for Tom and Lori.

Not wanting any camp participant to starve (it had been almost a whole three hours since they had dinner!), a snack was waiting for them all back in the dining hall. And everyone was now on their own. They could enjoy the snack while hanging out with friends; play board games or simply sit and talk. Instead of doing anything with others, Tom and Lori chose to go to the dining hall, get their snacks then walk back to their cottage to further discuss the evening session's content. "Why not?" they casually reasoned. But Lori's willingness to share was deeper than her casual demeanor implied. She really loved Tom. And during the evening speaker's presentation, Lori recalled a Sunday School lesson from her childhood. Specifically, from that lesson, she remembered what the apostle Peter wrote in the letter bearing his name. Her recollection was a simple phrase: "love each other deeply". That's exactly what she wanted to experience with Tom; deep love, even deeper than they had already expressed. She wondered if she could find the right words to convey to Tom her idea, better her hunger, for deep, caring-involvement in each other's lives.

Tom also wanted to share more than merely a typical marriage with Lori. Growing up, he reasoned, he had seen "typical" and wanted nothing of it. He didn't know the verse Lori remembered during the evening session, but he knew he wanted to love deeply. However, having been hurt and betrayed so many times he knew a herculean effort would be required to not give in to the fear of being betrayed again. So, before they even reached their cottage, both souls were preparing; both were asking for the Spirit's help to share and love deeply, even though Tom might not have described it that way. Their soulish preparation was already paying off for both of them through an increasing hunger-of-the-heart to risk being vulnerable. Fear of rejection would itself be rejected tonight.

Now propped up on their pillows in bed, as they shared deeply, they sensed a refreshing freedom with and acceptance of each other; a freedom they had never before experienced. In fact, they were discovering that they had never with anyone, in the entirety of their existence, shared so many memories from the deep corners of their souls. They delved into their personal self-concepts cautiously and with surprising detail, revealing the lies they had been told and believed; lies they felt had cheated them (until now) of true potential; lies which wounded and hurt deeply. They disclosed painful events from childhood, like the time Lori's kindergarten teacher made fun of her in front of the whole class…and the time Tom's parents took turns mocking his squeaky "junior high boy" voice; both parents were stoned at the time. With timidity defeated by raw courage they revealed the mental and emotional scars left by those wounds. As the minutes passed, they shared many more of the joys and tragedies that are common for those who live on this fallen planet.

Then Tom thought out loud, "It seems like we've only been sharing for a few minutes, but I have hunch it's been longer than that. What time is it?" They had been so caught up in sharing and risking together, crying and laughing together… it seemed like only minutes had passed when in fact hours had passed. They had climbed into bed planning to talk for a little bit then get some rest before breakfast and Sunday morning's first session. But the loving acceptance each received prompted an exhilarating cascade of self-disclosure; sleep seemed to flee from them. This exclusive time set aside for just them and their marriage had obviously energized their all-nighter.

About this time Lori noticed she was getting hungry. Tom too was hungry, and he also noticed that the windows in their cottage-in-the-woods were getting brighter as if someone was slowly turning a solar rheostat clockwise. They were both surprised that the sun indeed was rising. This dawn seemed way too premature and this night way too short as they realized they weren't even close to exploring all of their years of life prior to meeting each other. They thought it sadly odd that they, like many couples, made time for every other "urgent but not necessarily important" issue in their lives, but not for each other. Now, having sampled the relational riches of loving and sharing deeply, they were mutually resolved to keep "knowing each other" at the top of their things-to-do list.

Responding to the first light's ringing of the camp bell, while getting ready to go to the dining hall for breakfast, they each shared what they both were thinking: "Shouldn't we feel exhausted from a sleepless night of self-disclosure? Instead, we're feeling a strange yet wonderful sense of peace, energy, hope and expectancy, right? Life together is going to be great! But how much more is there to know about each other? Will we risk going deeper still?" Intuitively they each knew they wanted to be the other's most trusted confidant. And further inspired by the retreat speaker's instruction last night, they knew they bore the image of their Father and were therefore designed for profound relational intimacy. Resolute, both knew they were willing to make the time and take the risks necessary to invest in the second most important relationship they would ever experience. Lori and Tom were now, more than ever, committed to a life time of going deep.

Couples Daily Devotionals: Going Deep

Day One:

1. <u>Bible Reading</u>: The Amplified Version of Proverbs 18:24, says: "The man of too many friends (chosen indiscriminately) will be broken in pieces and come to ruin, But there is a (true, loving) friend who (is reliable and) sticks closer than a brother." (You can look up this version of the Bible on the internet via sites like biblegateway.com.)

   a. What does this "wisdom gem" tell you about indiscriminately choosing friends?

   b. What are some of the traits and qualities of a close friend? How might those traits and qualities be fostered in a spouse?

   c. What are some practical things you can do to further deepen your friendship?

   d. Do you as a couple have any close Christian friends? If yes, thank God. If not, what are you willing to do to gain close Christian friends?

   e. What are some topics that husbands/wives might stereotypically not want to share with their spouse? Why?

2. <u>Journal Time</u>: List at least two things you can do to deepen your friendship with each other. Schedule at least three times

this week you will talk about how to go deeper in your relationship/friendship.

3. Prayer Time: Pray for your friendship to go deeper. Pray for your children, grandchildren, nieces, and/or nephews, asking God to help them wisely choose their friends.

Day Two:
1. Bible Reading: John 15: 9-17.
   As spoken by Jesus, what are some of the qualities of true friends?
   a. Do you and your spouse share these friendship qualities and/or commitments? Explain your answer and what you personally are willing to do if any quality or commitment needs to be improved. Celebrate those areas you are doing well.

   b. What is the primary motive for being close friends? (cf. I John 4:7-8; I Corinthians 13)

   c. Name as many emotions as you can in 15 seconds. Some psychologists have lists that approach one hundred emotions. If you find it hard to list more than a dozen emotions, what might that say about our ability to express them? Perceive them?

   d. Friends care about every aspect of each other's well-being, including emotional health. When you share, be sure to include how you feel. How might your willingness or lack of willingness to share feelings be related to your assessment results?

    e. List some people you would like to have as closer friends. Ask God to help you develop those friendships and follow through on your desire to do so.

2. <u>Journal Time</u>: Record the qualities of true friends. Mark the ones you are doing well with a "check." Mark the ones that need improvement with a "box" indicating hopefully the box will have a "check" sooner than later.

3. <u>Prayer Time</u>: Ask the Holy Spirit to reveal to you any needed improvement areas in the friendship aspect of your marriage. In your journal record the things you "hear" or have a sense He is revealing to you. (If listening for the Spirit's voice is new to you, check out I Kings 19:12; John 10:27; Revelation 3:20; Jeremiah 1: 11,13).

Day Three:

1. <u>Bible Reading</u>: Psalms 147:3 says, "He (God) heals the broken hearted and binds up their wounds."

    a. Share an experience that has broken your heart, no matter how long ago it occurred. Why did it hurt so much? Which (all?) of the three basic human needs (acceptance, security, significance) were affected?

    b. Has God healed your broken heart? If needed, how might your mate also help in that process of healing?

    c. How might one's Motivational Value System® affect one's willingness (or hesitancy) to share?

    d. Some people might be afraid of sharing "deeply". I John 4:18 teaches us that "perfect drives out fear". How might this truth from I John mitigate a person's fear about sharing "deeply"?

    e. Read Ephesians 4:26. How might this truth help you deal with any anger associated with painful experiences?

2. <u>Journal Time</u>: Make a note that today you asked God (in your prayer time together today) to heal your spouse's heart.

3. <u>Prayer Time</u>: Pray for each other to be healed of any open relational/emotional wounds. If there is a relational issue that can be addressed, ask God for the courage and opportunity to do so. (read Romans 12:18)

Day Four:

1. <u>Bible Reading</u>: Proverbs 12:18 says, "The words of the reckless pierce like swords, but the tongue of the wise brings healing."

    a. What are reckless words? From your family of origin or childhood years, are there still some reckless words or derogatory words holding power over you?

    b. Based on this verse, is it true that "words can never hurt me"? Explain.

c. Ask each other, "Are you (we?) harboring any bitterness caused by reckless words?" Take time to identify them and to forgive each other. (Note: if you need some encouragement regarding forgiving one another refer to the lesson on Ephesians 4: 25-32 in the next session.)

d. Ask your spouse to personally identify some key "healing words" they might use.

2. Journal Time: For current and future use, make note of the healing words your spouse prefers to hear. In writing, commit to using them often to advance healing of old wounds and prevent new wounds from taking hold.

3. Prayer Time: Pray God's healing over your spouse using the healing words they shared.

Day Five:

1. Bible Reading: Proverbs 20:5 says, "A motive in the human heart is like deep water, and a person who has understanding draws it out." (God's Word translation). (Again, this and many other translations can be accessed through sites like biblegateway.com.)
   a. According to this verse, what kind of person can draw out the motive of another person's heart? Are you willing to help each other in this way? Express any hopes or fears this might cause you.

    b.   What resources are available to help a person learn how to "draw out" what is in a person's heart?

2.   <u>Journal Time</u>: What did you discover about each other today? Make notes and celebrate if you truly went deeper with God and each other.

3.   <u>Prayer Time</u>: Ask God to give you the courage to never hide from each other; to trust and be vulnerable. Pray that no fear-based "stronghold" will exist in your relationship. Pray also for the wisdom to help each other "draw out" what is in your heart.

Chapter Two
How to Fight Fair

Really?

She first saw him in the registration line at college. "Yes! Now I know I came to the right school!" Frank's demeanor, the way he carried himself, made her aware he was quite likely what she was looking for. Penny already knew what she and her future husband could achieve together.

Frank on the other hand was just having a good time, enjoying the people in line and the possibility of so many new friends. He was so engaged with those around him, he was surprised when he was called to step up to the next open spot at the counter to take care of his registration requirements. (Penny was now really glad she was hired a week before school started.) She was hoping he would be in her line. As it turned out, he was. And when their eyes met the first time, Frank was hooked, caught, and boated. It was only a matter of time and timing before they would have their first date…which of course Penny would plan and pursue.

On that first date, they went to a museum of fine art. But they really experienced it through different "eyes." For instance:

- The vast array of portraits, landscapes, and seascapes caused Frank to wonder about their creators.
- Penny wondered what it took to build the place and how many people to run it.
- Frank was in tune with the carefree-timelessness of the environment; he had plenty of room to talk with Penny as well as the well-trained staff.
- Penny loved how comfortable Frank was with her and with everyone else. Even strangers liked chatting with Frank. Yet, she couldn't help but wonder: Do I have first place in his heart? Is this relationship headed anywhere?

Impatient to a mild degree, Penny, as they paused to sit on a mahogany bench in front of a classic masterpiece, gently placed her head on Frank's shoulder while also reaching for his hand. She felt so much affirmation from being the one who had apparently conquered his heart.

Frank sensed her advance was appropriate; he loved how self-assured Penny was. Her confidence gave him a sense of calm, like an anchor to his soul. And it was nice not having to work so hard to guess what would impress her. She was pretty clear about what she did and didn't like, and that made the relationship so much easier for Frank, though it did challenge his sense of romance. (To himself Frank thought, "Should romance be this predictable? Romance wasn't supposed to be like this, or was it?")

Some might call it a perfect match of opposites. And…their dates became more frequent. Their knowledge of each other's likes and dislikes increased. Their quirks became familiar and treasured. Their growing up years and family histories were shared, including all the joys, achievements, disappointments, lies and even wounds. Now, this relationship was heading somewhere serious!

As the weeks turned into months, Penny began to wonder if Frank was ever going to ask her to marry him. She wondered if he felt the same as she did. For one so self-confident, she began to fear she was becoming doubtful about this relationship becoming a lifetime union. She began to wonder if she should take the lead and ask Frank to marry her. As unnatural as patience was to her, she did indeed wait. Eventually with a perfectly planned set up, Frank surprised her and through his profoundly felt tears, invited her to be his one-and-only. Penny accepted, of course, with a tone that faintly implied, "What took you so long?" Though her tone was perceived by Frank, he let it slide. Swept up in a flood of joy and relief, Frank took Penny in his arms and held her as if to never let her go.

Were they married "happily ever after?" Does that really ever happen other than in fairy tales?

Around the 20-month mark of their marriage, they began to fall out of love with "being in love." Reality started to set in. Some behaviors weren't so cute anymore. Bills, schedules, friends, higher education, extended family, careers, all came at them like rounds from the turret of a WWI biplane. Sometimes the shots weren't from those outside the marriage, but from each other. To say the least, it was disheartening to both.

Penny would regularly say marginally hurtful things to Frank. Evaluating his ongoing need to be relationally "connected" or his attempts at personal disclosures, it was not uncommon for her to respond with a blunt comment like, "I didn't think men were like that." Then to herself she would reason, "Aren't most behaviors gender specific?"

Frank felt that her "chippy" quips challenged his manliness. It wasn't uncommon for him to say nothing in response to her short but not-so-sweet put-downs. Her verbal gut punches caused him to seek seclusion even if it was only in his mind. When in pensive retreat, Frank would entertain thoughts like, "Does she really care about me? Does she have some innate drive to control everyone; maybe the whole world? God help us if she ever does!"

You guessed it, conflict was a constant in their marriage and it could get quite ugly at times.

When really pushed, Frank would go through a progression of personality changes; from mister nice-guy, to reserved, to Godzilla spewing verbal fire and brimstone that could rival Pompeii's cataclysm.

When Penny was pushed she would go from the woman-in-charge to a muted withdrawal that Frank found perplexing. One minute she was nearly red-faced with what she called "being engaged." (And when engaged, she could talk 90 miles an hour with gusts up to 120!) But then it seemed like the next minute she would become quiet, like her verbal machine gun had run out of rounds.

He would think, "How does that make sense?! After all, aren't women always supposed to have a massive reserve of readily available verbiage? Did I unwittingly marry a crazy woman?"

They found that retreating from each other was usually a successful strategy for cooling off; but it resolved nothing. And during most self-imposed truces they would both be taunted by dark thoughts: Had they misread each other during courtship? Or maybe even worse, had they deceived each other during courtship? Was this marriage a huge mistake? Was there another person out there somewhere that was better suited for each of them (even though they weren't exactly sure what "better" meant)? Was divorce just over the horizon but moving fast like a category-five hurricane, devastation included? Would it end like supposedly half of all marriages do? These and dozens of other unanswerable questions raced through both their minds.

Their relationship disintegrated to the point that they spoke to each other only when necessary. Often, in the tense silence, they each rehashed their allegations and re-processed each other's responses. It was like they were in some kind of mental house-of-mirrors; no matter which way they turned, from every possible angle, they individually saw and heard themselves again and again; what they saw and heard wasn't pretty. Neither was pleased with their thoughts or actions. The one thought that haunted both their minds were, "How in the world did we get here?"

After one of their too-common-these-days "fight nights," when sleep was impossible, they were both staring in icy silence at the ceiling, and then one of them began to talk. But the conversation wasn't helpful and didn't go very far. The words and attitudes that emerged only served to make things worse. A sense of anger, hopeless sorrow, confusion and cluelessness seemed to fill the room and neither one knew where to go next. Silence resumed. It was as if someone pushed the "pause" button mid-fight. When the pause was over, and the fight rejoined, Frank calmly offered what turned out to be his last verbal jab for the night. In response, Penny merely turned her face to the wall and barely muttered, "Really?!"

They had a hard time sleeping having been amped-up by their fighting; there was too much adrenalin in their systems. But eventually sleep did come. Their minds, tired from trying to one-up each other's verbal attacks and counter-attacks, finally succumbed to exhaustion.

The next day, a Saturday, they awoke warm and nestled closely together under their comforting, warm flannel sheets. Penny's eyes opened first. Inches away from his face, she was staring right at Frank. He was starting to stir but wasn't fully awake yet. Penny could have pried herself out of his arms, but she chose to stay in hopes of making amends. When Frank's eyes finally did pop open, his first sight of the day was Penny's hopeful eyes; it melted his heart. The anger of last night was gone but not forgotten. Both were tentative about their next words fearing they might trigger another round of fighting. Neither one of them was up to that, and they never again wanted to have a fight that horrid.

Frank finally spoke first. His anger was receding, but still active. He mustered the humility and courage to say, "I am sorry, Penny. I don't ever want to do that again. Will you forgive me?" "For what?" she replied. She wanted specifics! But as quickly as the provocative, interrogating words were out of her mouth, she knew it was a mistake. She quickly recovered saying, "Forget that for now. I shouldn't have said that, not now. It's just that, I don't know how to fight with you; how to fight fair, I mean. I know we have issues that need to be resolved, but I would rather it be a win-win situation. Thank you for apologizing, it means a lot. Will you forgive me for the pain I caused you?"

Frank looked at Penny curiously while wondering if her "thank you" and apology somehow implied his apology had been accepted; it was still unclear. Plus, he was wondering if her admission of guilt was sincere or simply an attempt to establish another fragile truce.

After her apology, Penny was hoping for a healing response from Frank, even though she wasn't sure what it would look, feel, or sound like.

Neither received what they thought they should. So, instead, they just looked at each other not knowing what to say next. It was awkward.

Fearful of saying something that would provoke each other, they temporarily avoided conversation. Neither knew how to resolve the issues of last night's fight or heal the wounds it caused; there were still so many relational land mines just waiting to be stepped on. And honestly, neither were really sure <u>how</u> to apologize nor how to respond to the other's apology. In hopes that one of them would somehow intuitively know what to do if given enough time, they stayed a bit longer in their luxuriously warm bed. They found out later that during this silence, both were wondering something like, "How do we resolve the issues and truly forgive so we don't ever fight like that again? How do we not keep a record of wrongs; a record that likely will become ammunition for our next fight? How do we effectively apologize?"

Penny knew she had to get up and address the day's demands. Finally, she got out of bed, but didn't move far. She turned to Frank who was now sitting on the edge of the bed, elbows on his knees, head in hands. As a possible solution to their stalemate, she compassionately said, "Would you be willing to get some help? I mean for us to get some help? I want this relationship to thrive. I don't want us to become two bitter, miserable people who feel stuck with each other. This is supposed to be a loving commitment, not a life-sentence. I love you!" Frank stood up then stretched with great animation that included a loud yawn. His aloof demeanor belied the ache in his soul. To Penny's question he replied with effort, "I'm sorry, I may seem like I don't care but I do care deeply." Defensively he admitted, "I sometimes struggle with my own pride. I know the rules for football, but I don't know the rules for fighting fair with my wife. I was never taught. How can that possibly be? Honey, yeah, we are going to get some help. I'll even do the research to find us some good help. It will be the first thing on my to-do list today, ok? In fact, while online the other day, I read that at our church tomorrow there is a class about fighting fair. It's been a while since we have gone together, how 'bout we begin again starting with that class?"

Penny walked around to his side of the bed. She reached for both of his hands, took them then moved them behind her back hopefully guiding him to embrace her. It worked. Then, reaching up to his cheeks, she held his face in her hands while affectionately looking into his eyes and simultaneously wondering what he was thinking. Sensing no resistance from Frank, she moved in closer to kiss him but stopped just short of his lips. Frank closed the remaining distance between them. The kiss that followed was sincere and appropriately long. When they pulled back far enough to again lovingly look into each other's eyes, they both intuitively knew they had resolved to weather this storm and prepare better for the next. To each their gaze communicated partial recall of their vows: "For better or for worse." Leaving no doubt, they gave words to what their embrace, eyes and kiss had just spoken. Reassuring each other, they mutually expressed, "This is a life-time commitment. Let's make it great. We have got to learn how to fight fair, really!"

Couples' Daily Devotionals: How to Fight Fair

Day one:

1. <u>Bible Reading</u>:
   Proverbs 18:1says, "An unfriendly person pursues selfish ends and against all sound judgment starts quarrels."
   a. How is a person who starts quarrels depicted in this verse? So, is it ever ok to start a quarrel? Which one of you might be more inclined to start a quarrel? Finish a quarrel? How might this be related to your Conflict Sequence®? (Note: One's Conflict Sequence® can be discovered by taking the online assessment known as the Strength Deployment Inventory*.)

   b. Proverbs 18:21 (MSG) says, "Words kill, words give life; they're either poison or fruit—you choose." Can you list any poisonous words you use to push your spouse's proverbial buttons? Why do you do use them? What words can you use with your spouse to produce "life" or "good fruit"?

2. <u>Journal Time</u>: Take time to note each other's Conflict Sequence®. Also, record any words to use or avoid when you are in conflict with each other.

3. Prayer Time: Ask God to help you both have sound
    judgement, so you can know when it is best to cover an
    offense and when it is best to fight fair.

    Day Two:
1. Bible Reading: 1 Peter 4:8 says, "Above all, love each other
    deeply, because love covers over a multitude of sins."
    a. "Covering" is different than "covering up". "Covering"
        refers to overlooking an offense. However, if something
        is bothering you and you can't let it go, you might be
        "covering up" rather than "covering" the offense. As
        Ephesians 4:25 states: "What this adds up to, then, is this:
        no more lies, no more pretense. Tell your neighbor the
        truth. In Christ's body we're all connected to each other,
        after all. When you lie to others, you end up lying to
        yourself."

    b. Do either or both of you "accommodate" when in
        conflict? For example: saying, "Oh, it's ok." "No big
        deal, it only hurt a little bit, etc." …. when it's actually
        not ok and the offense was big and real. How does
        accommodating help or hinder your relationship? How
        might "accommodating" be mistaken for "agreement"?

2. Journal Time: Record as prayer requests any relationships
    that need God's healing touch. Be sure to come back to this
    page to record the peace you see God bringing to you and
    your family as a result of this request.

3. <u>Prayer Time</u>: Ask the Holy Spirit to give you courage to reconcile those relationships you can and to be at peace with those you can't…and to know the difference. (cf. Romans 12:18 "If it is possible, as far as it depends on you, live at peace with everyone.")

Day Three:

1. <u>Bible Reading</u>: II Timothy 2: 23 says, "Don't have anything to do with foolish and stupid arguments, because you know they produce quarrels."
   a. Can you identify any quarrel producing topics in your marriage? (e.g. "politics".)

   b. What does God's Word teach us to do with "foolish and stupid" arguments?

   c. What would be some wise ways to handle the quarrel producing topics you identified?

2. <u>Journal Time</u>: Are there quarrel producing issues or topics in your relationship? List them including some strategies to help you keep them from producing foolish arguments.

3. <u>Prayer Time</u>: Pray especially for those family members that are prone to be argumentative. Ask God to give them a heart for peace and wisdom.

Day Four:

1. Bible Reading: James 4:1 says, "What causes fights and quarrels among you? Don't they come from your desires that battle within you?"

    a. What are some of the fight causing, ungodly desires that battle within you? Your marriage?

    b. Romans 8:6 says, "The mind governed by the flesh is death, but the mind governed by the Spirit is life and peace." How might this truth compel you to replace ungodly desires with godly desires?

    c. When you are in conflict, are you more inclined to accommodate, analyze or assert? What might this tell you about your "desires"?

2. Journal Time: Take a moment to list those ungodly "desires" that battle within you. In order to measure your progress, agree to refer back to this page in thirty days.

3. Prayer Time: Pray together asking God to help you conquer any ungodly desires in your marriage.

Day Five:

1. Bible Reading: Colossians 3:13 says, "Bear with each other and forgive one another if any of you has a grievance against someone. Forgive as the Lord forgave you." Colossians 3:13 (cf. Ephesians 4:32, Matthew 6:14-15)

    a. In what manner has God forgiven us? How are we to model His example with each other? Is there forgiveness you need to extend to your spouse? Will you do so? How will they know you have done so?

b. Forgiveness has to do with the present and the past. Trust has to do with the present and the future. How might these two issues be confused?

c. It has been stated that withholding forgiveness is a tactic used to protect one's soul. Do you agree or disagree? How might this protective action be to the benefit and/or detriment of one's soul?

2. <u>Journal Time</u>: Record this date as a day of "freedom" from any wrongs that are now forgiven. Psalms 103:12 says, "As far as the east is from the west, so far has He removed our transgressions from us." When the Enemy seeks to remind you of wrongs committed against you, run to God for strength to stay "free" from the power and tyranny of forgiven/cancelled sins either you or your spouse have committed.

3. <u>Prayer Time</u>:

a. Pray for each other to be quick to forgive and slow to take an offense.

b. Pray through I Corinthians 13: 4-13a, asking God to help you both be more loving. (Note the action-words/verbs of love.) "Love is patient, love is kind. It does not envy, it does not boast, it is not proud. It does not dishonour others, it is not self-seeking, it is not easily angered, it keeps no record of wrongs. Love does not delight in evil but rejoices with the truth. It always protects, always trusts, always hopes, always perseveres. Love never fails." I Corinthians 13:4-13b

Chapter Three
Spiritual Warfare

Money!

Rich woke up, sort of, in a sweat. What a restless night. He turned over to gaze through sleepy eyes at the glowing red numbers on his digital alarm clock. To his bleary eyes it looked like an imaginary monster, the kind conjured by a child's imagination. It seemed like it had crawled out from under his bed, perched itself on the bedside night stand, then mercilessly begun staring at him. How long had it been patiently waiting there for just the perfect frightening moment? Were its menacing, crimson, creepy, digital-eyes once again taunting him with these implied sing-song words, "It's 2:22 a.m. Time for an anxiety attack!"

Rich was now somewhere in-between the no man's land of sort-of-asleep and not-quite-awake. Why was his heart racing? Was he dreaming or was this ephemeral battle real? Drowsily he discovered his stomach was churning due to this latest bout with his heightened (imaginary?) concerns. Being half-awake, he couldn't determine if this attack was just a thought or a person. A thousand thoughts suddenly seemed to compete for primary position in his consciousness. Then out of nowhere, in some alcove of his mind, a picture from a 60's era family photo album began to form. He saw himself seated in the church of his youth. His mother was next to him, and he wasn't sure who was next to her nor who was on the other side of him. But he could, in the fog of that microsecond thought, hear singing. He sensed that the congregation was harmonizing a chorus which sounded like, "Leaning on the everlasting arms, safe and secure from all alarms." In the foggy quietness of his not-yet-fully-awake mind he thought, "Where did that memory come from and why now?"

Processing these thoughts caused Rich to wake up a bit more. So, was he currently sensing a residual evil presence in the room? Were his teeth and fists clenched from the tension he felt, or was he ready to fight someone, or was it some "thing"? "It happened again!" he thought. His unspoken words contained a sense of surprise wrapped in anger wrapped in fear wrapped in guilt. "And at the same time of night!"

The previous night, before going to bed, Rich and Karen had had a short but very injurious fight. The emotional wounds Karen inflicted on Rich only deepened his "I have to fix this!" guilt. So, he had gone to bed knowing he had to come up with some fair and equitable solution for everyone involved in the recent crisis. He had to solve this situation for his wife, his kids, his grandkids and maybe even his former boss, if that were possible. Rich felt the weight of the knowledge that he was supposed to be the provider and that he was supposed to be the perfect master planner. He was supposed to have their financial portfolio all wrapped up in a nice package for loving presentation to Karen at about this season in their marriage. Well, he did have a provision plan, but it evaporated, "poof", when he lost his job a few years shy of what his plan had called for. He reasoned, "If things could just settle down for a bit, I am sure I can solve this situation somehow."

Then even though he had had little deep-sleep, having wrestled with his pillow and blankets most of the night, he thought, "It has to be about time to get out of bed, but for what? I don't have a job, so there's nowhere I have to be." As he continued to lay there covered in sweat, the replay feature in his brain played over and over the previous night's painful fight with Karen. And now, in the aftermath of what should have been a time of sound-sleep but was in fact a time of hardly-asleep, his heart was pounding again. Its throbbing was a result of the unjust things Karen had said and the more accurate responses he could have argued if only he were as quick thinking as Karen. Rich's tachycardia was also caused by their ever-looming lack of funds, at least it looked that way.

Rich (inside the corridors of his mind he laughed at the irony of his name) rolled over on his bed then looked again at the digital clock on his night stand. As he sought to focus and read the time he wondered, "Are those digital red numbers now merely telling me it is 2:28 a.m. or were they a moment ago, actually someone's eyes? Is what happened during the night simply another bad dream or was something else going on?" Now wide awake, staring at the ceiling, his anger simmering again, he recalled that just a few hours ago Karen had hurt him, badly.

Karen, his wife of 40-plus years, had been asking Rich a bunch of questions about their current financial status. She reacted, "Now that your employment situation has so drastically changed, are we going to be able to buy food?" She was trying to choose her words carefully; to be tactful. "Of course!" Rich defensively responded. He went on to tell her of a friend in whom he had confided, who knew their circumstances and counseled, "No one is going to let you go hungry, even if you don't have enough money to buy food." For some reason he couldn't quite identify, or even admit, Rich was barely comforted by his friend's offer of assistance.

Rick and Karen's pre-bedtime fight was brief but it had caused a high degree of damage that was hard for even Rick to explain. Words meant so much to him, and this time Karen's words were as reckless as ever but exceptionally penetrating. Were her words energized by some evil force? Or was the energizing in the hearing (Rich's hearing to be exact)? He was more sensitive than usual having been deeply wounded when he was poorly treated then recently fired from the company he had served for years. Whatever the source of the damage, it was real. They went to bed angry and found only moments of fitful sleep.

When it was finally a reasonable hour to get out bed, but barely a few hours after the 2:22 a.m. "attack" on Rich, they both started their day. Without saying much to each other and from different bathrooms in their house, they drearily shuffled into the kitchen. As they ate breakfast, they picked up where they left off; the previous night's fight was resumed.

What they couldn't have possibly seen was someone else in the kitchen with them. It was some host, unknown to them, just aching to witness another round of fighting between Rich and Karen. He wanted them to fight but hoped they would resolve nothing. He predicted an injurious fight while forecasting another resultant "draw". It wasn't hard for this peace-killer's expectations to be fulfilled. True, this "someone" was trying hard to destroy not only the peace in their home but their marriage as well. Rich and Karen's circumstantial fear and doubt made easy this specter's mission to kill, steal and destroy.

To this "presence", the relational damage Rich and Karen inflicted on each other was so wickedly delicious and selfishly satisfying it just _had_ to be unresolved and indefinitely continued. So….

As they entered the kitchen, he was already present. He was coiled like a spring-loaded trap just waiting to seize any opportunity to provoke Rich and Karen towards another round of verbal combat. He would not have to wait long. Unsure of their true standing before the Father, their damaged egos provided just the opening the hideous creature needed. The bell for round two was rung.

Now at the breakfast table, Karen verbally advanced and Rich pensively withdrew. It was almost like he was having an out-of-body experience, watching himself. He could hear Karen's voice droning on in the background of his thoughts; but his mind was surging (albeit analytically) with myriad "woulda-coulda-shouldas." These waves of self-condemning thoughts kept pounding the beachhead of his soul. Thoughts like:

- "If I only had compromised my principles!" Followed by, "Uh, no, I couldn't have done that.
- "If I could have only known the motivation my boss was assigning to my behavior; boy, did she get that wrong! If only she had asked me to explain. Or was it that I misinterpreted _her_ motivation? But how could we know what was going on inside each other without some honest disclosure? But such disclosure would probably have been quite awkward and likely accelerated me getting terminated.

I don't even know the right way to ask in order to get answers to these questions!

- "The company leadership often talked about how much they valued and even loved their employees, but the abrupt way they treated me then fired me says otherwise. The obviously illegal way my dismissal was executed makes me feel, what? rejected, insignificant, yeah probably both and more. Maybe I should have been more.... well, more 'someone else' other than me? But is that even possible for any extended period of time?"

- Rich's thoughts continued on a different trail now. "And when it comes to others buying food for us, I don't want to be someone's welfare project." He was now self-righteously disgusted by the thought of his friend's offer to buy food. "I should be buying food for others, not others for me. But when have I ever bought food for others?"

For some strange reason Karen's voice was gaining volume, at least in his perception she was getting louder. And now he was "back" with most of his focus on her monologue.

From her side of the table Karen nearly shouted, "Richard! Are you even listening to me?" Honestly his answer should have been "no," but having heard her use his full first name, he knew better than to volunteer that response. Karen was in full attack mode. Rich wasn't going to take it this time so he got up from his chair then walked the few steps to the kitchen sink. There he noisily rinsed his cereal bowl. He rotated 180 degrees then leaned against the kitchen counter. He wasn't about to go back to the table and, no he hadn't really been listening. (Karen had correctly interpreted his not-listening demeanor at the table.) And now at the sink, he was leaning back against the counter, arms crossed but with the fingers of his right-hand fidgeting restlessly in an attempt to cover his lips. Karen couldn't help but silently interpret his posture as defiant. Inside her soul she thought, "Oh good grief ... that fidgeting; yep, he is all negative once again." She was indeed annoyed, rather "super-charged" and annoyed!

Overdoing her verbal persuasiveness, Karen now was raising her voice in what would be another futile attempt to regain his attention. Volume, she just knew, was an effective tactic to help Rich reacquire focus when they fought. As her voice became louder, she was at the same time in her mind's war-room, observing Rich's tactics. It seemed to her whenever they fought, Rich would just start distancing himself. She could sense and even see it every time. His behavior could be likened to a stone skipping across a pond. Each skip seemed to reveal a different person or was it just a different attitude? "Yeah, attitude…that was probably it," she decided. That observation reminded her to have her reserve verbal responses ready for his inevitably delayed counterattack no matter how far in the future it might come.

She could already envision his forthcoming behavioral changes; they could come on in a seeming instant. He could change from calm engagement to condescending "whatever you want" or mock, whiny "yes dear" comments. Oooh that last one really forced her to be so mad! Next, he would start in with the frustration-laced mutterings about "fairness, calmness and timing." His rejoinders included phrases and sometimes even whole sentences like: "That's not fair!" Or he could utter the most annoying command to "just calm down." She always reasoned, "I am calm. We are just finally really getting into it, whatever the 'it' du jour might be!"

Karen knew that Rich's "skips" were usually predictable. But there was one incident she chose never to forget. Somewhere around 20 years ago a rare "skip on the pond" included shouting back at her like she had never heard him shout before and he was standing so close. At first, she thought they were finally really getting some honest, active engagement. Then she got quite scared by his uncharacteristically menacing presence. Had she ever really recovered from that incident?

Though hardly perceptible, Karen seemed to rapidly shake her head side to side in order to forget that horrible encounter and reapply her focus to the contest before her. To herself she thought, "Why is my thinking so fuzzy?" She sensed that Rich was now mentally here again. So, she reasoned it was time to verbally up the ante. She advanced with one of her typical interrogations, like the closing statement of a trial lawyer. (From a high corner in the kitchen, the "host" was maliciously grinning while affirming what he sensed was going to be an especially damaging barrage from Karen. His sense was correct.)

She peppered Rich with comments and questions:

- "What if we can't find affordable health insurance once your current coverage lapses?" (That one was a tough question for Rich to logically answer.)

- "What if we have to make a lot of standard of living changes?" (How could Rich answer such a broad, general question? It made him anxious just thinking about finding the right words to express an intelligent response.)

- "How could we save on our utility bills? What if we are too hot in the summer and too cold in the winter?" ("Summer? - cold drinks! Winter? - jackets and blankets! Duh! Come on now, Rich," he said to himself. "Being sarcastic won't help, but when she comes at me like this, it sure is self-righteously fun.")

- "Would Rich be willing to give up his cable TV?" (It wasn't that TV was any real source of comfort these days, especially the financial news. He knew the old adage, "If it bleeds it leads," but still he was a news junky, bad news and all. Nope, TV would stay, even if he had to collect aluminum cans to keep it!)

- "What if they didn't have enough money to continue socializing with their longtime friends?" (Even to herself, Karen thought, "Friends? Do we really have any close friends we can count on in times of trouble?")

- "What if we lose our home?" (Rich thought, "You always said, 'As long as we are together it doesn't matter where we live or what we live in.' Now it matters?")

- "What if we can't ever afford to retire? What if we have to be greeters at the local 'big box' store? What if we can't treat our grandkids to ice cream? What if we can't travel liked we had planned?"

They discovered anew that this mental/verbal walk down "what-if-alley," that trashed, chaotic, dark, cold, damp, fear-infested alley, was and is really depressing.

At some point, Karen took a break from her what-if-laced closing argument. Rich finally broke his silence to cautiously remind her: 1) They had faithfully but not perfectly managed what

God had entrusted to them through the years. 2) They had paid for the lion's share of their five kids' college educations and weddings. 3) They had sacrificed through the child rearing years by having Karen stay at home with the children. ("Your request," he reminded her.) 4) They had made significant charitable contributions. 5) They did have some savings, but definitely not enough.

Then to himself he thought, "Enough? Have we ever defined what 'enough' is? And surely God is not going to abandon us now, right? Or would He?" Robbed of his sense of security, insecurity was now raging through his mind and causing waves of near nausea to churn in his stomach. (The "host" was relishing Rich's misery.) Rich wondered, "Are we being punished for my confessed but recurring sins? On the other hand, should the blame for their circumstances lie with her? No, that couldn't be. Karen was mostly a saint." His inner thoughts told him that she was good and he was bad; he must be the problem. Even though he had faithfully walked with God for years, he was still susceptible to that niggling thought about being, what? an orphan? Yes, that is a good description, an orphan who must beg for God's favor. But how much begging was enough? He knew he had to be exceedingly righteous in order to receive God's blessings yet being perfect seemed always beyond his grasp. Rich knew, he just knew, as he had been taught all his life, God's blessings are conditional upon one's performance. Oh, he believed in grace but, though he knew it not, his was a more legalistic version of grace.

Sensing his thoughts, the ghoul smirked while in his native tongue he suggested sinister subtleties to Rich's mind. "Yes, 'grace', but you must earn it, Rich. Preserve that thinking, it is so piously humble."

Karen didn't respond to Rich's five-point attempt to assure her that all was well. She merely stared at him for an uncomfortably long moment, then left the kitchen. In their bedroom she finished getting herself ready for another day of job hunting. She reentered the kitchen, walked past Rich, exiting through the door that led to the garage. (Again, neither one stopped to think about praying together before parting. Again, a full day would pass without the vast resources that come with the Spirit's empowerment.) Karen had entered her car then driven off without directly saying a single word to Rich. What she didn't know was this: by a nod, from the lead on-site spirit, an invisible malevolent minion was deployed to keep her company.

Back in the kitchen, the demon assigned to Rich affected a short-lived and very sinister smile. He was pleased with his accomplishments so far. He knew this fight was not resolved. He did not want it to be resolved. For him Rich and Karen's constant fighting was so deliciously, wickedly enjoyable he just had to keep it festering. And now that that the couple had parted without any peace or solutions, the fiend knew it was going to be a long miserable day for both of them. Mission accomplished.

When she was gone, Rich analytically wondered to himself, "Is it possible my nightmares are somehow connected to these intense skirmishes I am now having daily with Karen? Are they connected? And, will I ever stop having all this self-condemning self-talk, and the inevitable bad dreams that follow? This time the fights and harrowing nightmare were about money! What topic will the 'night monster' bring to my dreams next time?" "And whenever we fight," Rich reasoned, "it gets eerily 'weird' in our house. Is there a monster in our home? Should we have dedicated this house with some kind of blessing when we moved in a year ago?" These and a dozen other seemingly unanswerable questions were aggressively rotating round the race track of his mind.

Battle weary, Rich retreated to the den where the internet was accessible. At his computer he began to search for some employment leads and maybe some answers to what he was beginning to call his "monster" questions. As he leafed through one site after another, false-comfort was offered from a variety of vacuous venues. He was clueless to the subtlety of the cruel traps being laid; the enemy's "tried and true" sinister strategies were in full-implementation. Rich had no idea that in realms unseen, he, better "they" were being followed.

Couples' Daily Devotionals: Spiritual Warfare

Day One:

1. <u>Bible Reading:</u> Luke 4:1-13. How did Satan use the "Three Passions of the Soul"** (acceptance, security, significance) to tempt Jesus?

    a. Which of the three "passions" does the Enemy regularly use to personally attack you? What strategy(s) can you use to help you stand against his personal attack on you?

    b. What does Luke 4:13 tell you about Satan's "ways"? His "patient" warfare against us?

2. <u>Journal Time:</u> List a least one way the enemy regularly attacks you and/or your marriage. Can you record a winning strategy? (Examples: Memorize applicable promises from the Bible and/or print them out and post them on your refrigerator or bathroom mirror. Which of the "three passions of the soul" does the Enemy most often attack?)

3. <u>Prayer Time:</u> Pray for each other to have victory over the enemy today and every day. In order to be fully empowered for God's purposes and glory this day, ask Him to fill you with His Holy Spirit. If you have children pray this for them too; and for your grandchildren, nieces and nephews.

Day Two:

1. <u>Bible Reading:</u> Read Ephesians 6:11-12. The "full armor of God" is listed in verse 13ff. Which of the listed pieces of

spiritual armor are most significant to you? Why? Today, what is a good way to practice "putting on God's armor"? How might you "leave it on"?

2. <u>Journal Time:</u> Note the armor you described as "most significant" to you and your spouse and the reason why. Also, make a note of your answer to the "how to put/keep" it on.

3. <u>Prayer Time:</u> Ask God to help each of you walk in the power and protection of His mighty armor today.

Day Three:
1. <u>Bible Reading</u>: II Cor. 2: 10-11. In your opinion, what connection might there be between not forgiving others and Satan "outwitting us"? Do you have any unforgiveness between the two of you? Will you resolve to forgive and do so?

2. <u>Journal Time</u>: Record a commitment to each other to keep "short accounts" (to not keep a record of wrongs). Next to your written commitment write I Corinthians 13: 5b which says, "…love keeps no record of wrongs". If you are struggling with forgiving each other, review the chapter on "How to Fight Fair."

3. Prayer Time: Ask God to help you both be "peace makers" (Matthew 5:9); to give you both a heart to forgive as well as extend forgiveness to each other.

Day Four:
1. Bible Reading: I Peter 5:8. Do you think you do a good job of "being alert" to the enemy's attacks on you? Your marriage? Your family? If you need improvement, what might be a good first step? (Examples: Simply identify "how" you think you are being tempted at the very moment the temptation hits. "How" or "where" might include: time of day/night, location, topics, activities etc.)

2. Journal Time: Make notes of where/how you think the Enemy may be attacking you and/or your marriage. Why? Often times, identifying the problem is half the battle.

3. Prayer Time: Ask God to give you courage and discernment to identify and resist the enemy's attacks. See Ephesians 3: 14-20, 6:18-20.

Day Five:
1. Bible Reading: Luke 22:31-32. In this passage, Jesus warned Peter that Satan really wanted to mess him up. Jesus assured Peter that he would survive this attack.
   a. What did Jesus tell Peter to do with the lessons learned from Satan's attack? (FYI: Neil Anderson's

book, "The Bondage Breaker" is a great resource for answering your questions regarding spiritual warfare.)

    b. What might be some good ways to share your personal experience(s) with each other? With your children/grandchildren, nieces/nephews?

2. <u>Journal Time</u>: Make a list of family members you want to share your spiritual warfare experiences with. Record some "do this by" dates alongside each name then write "done" once you have shared with each person listed.

3. <u>Prayer Time</u>: Ask God to help you have victory over the Enemy and for the opportunity(s) to share your experience(s) with those listed in your journal.

Chapter Four
Devotional Times for Couples

"Quiet" Time

When they first met, Roland was teaching a Bible study for college-age students on campus. The response was significant. Valerie was one of the co-eds in attendance and wow! did she love his teaching...or did she love him?

Somewhere along the way they actually talked to each other one-on-one. To this day they aren't sure when that first encounter was. Maybe it happened at the drink-bar the night they had a "pizza/invite a friend" party. Anyway, here they were alone in a room full of people giving exclusive attention to each other. Their discussion revolved mainly around last week's teaching and "what are we covering tonight?" His knowledge of God's Word, compassion for the lost, and desire to serve the King confirmed to her that she was definitely falling in love with this amazing man of God.

Roland on the other hand was stereotypically clueless of her interest. He finally got a clue and decided Valerie was not someone he wanted to let get away. Subtly, at least he thought he was subtle, he began to arrange things so they could have more time together. For instance, he found her a job off campus. She had had a desk job on campus in the men's dorm...checking out sports equipment to would-be athletes. Roland thought, "There has to be some way to get her away from my competition!" He managed to find a live-in nanny job for her, which just happened to be right next door to where his older brother lived. It was a money-making, money-saving, relationship-advancing opportunity and answered-prayer, for both of them.

Meanwhile, their college Bible study was growing. Relationship doors were opening for Ro and Val. They studied God's Word together at the group's weekly gathering and they studied as often as they could one-on-one. When they did meet, their prayer times were rich. They would sing and worship together; each was gifted to play the guitar and lead worship. Even though they hadn't had any formal training in couples' devotional times, God was blessing their spiritual times together and their relationship. Yes, they were indeed falling in love. That was obvious to everyone. It became common for people in their study group to encourage them with prompts like, "You guys would make a great couple!" Like they weren't one already? What their friendly observers meant was, "You two should get married." There was little doubt in Val's and Ro's minds that they would indeed get married. It was just a simple matter of when Ro would "pop" the question. He finally did. She joyfully agreed. It would be hard to imagine a happier couple.

After the wedding, they kept involved in church, but the necessary completion of their college educations, and their demanding careers, got in the way of time with God and each other. When kids were added to the mix, time together with God as a couple was an even rarer commodity.

They tried a variety of devotional guides for couples, but none seemed to capture their long-term attention.

They tried quick, "just takes seconds" daily devotionals. Well, that was better than nothing, they reasoned, and it often fit their morning routine. At least it was an attempt.

In a commendable effort to beef up their marriage, they went to a SoulmatesForLife weekend retreat. They were encouraged and challenged. They mutually acknowledged the hunger they had to seek God together. Their resulting promise to re-establish a devotional time together worked, for a few weeks. However, that promise lapsed when routine took over, once again.

Soon Val began to wonder, "What happened to the man of God I married? Why don't we study the Word together anymore? We don't even read it together anymore. And I hope no one even asks us about our prayer times! Those are pretty much gone too. What prayer time we do have happens mainly when we are hungry and hovering over food. I want reflection and meditation to be part of our prayer time. I want to choose the right words to express my heartfelt gratitude to my heavenly Father. But when I take the time to do so, Roland seems to have some mental 'shot clock' ticking in his head that buzzes when he determines time is up. He can get almost irritable with me when we pray. I want to spend time waiting on the Holy Spirit. But he seems to have some kind of internal GPS that just goes somewhere other than wherever we are when we pray. I sure hope it doesn't take some crisis to get us back on track."

And their lack of spiritual life together didn't leave Roland out of the condemning self-talk and ensuing guilt either. His thoughts were along the lines of, "I want to study the Word with her, but she seems to get lost in minutiae while I am trying to get to the main points, and finish. I mean, I have an outline of the whole chapter mapped out in my head, when she hasn't even moved past reading the first phrase of the first sentence. I do want to pray together more. But when we pray together, if I stop to give her an opportunity she just sits there in silence for minutes on end saying nothing ... at least out loud she says nothing ... so how is that praying together? I sometimes have to nudge her to be sure she is awake and knows it's her turn. I have learned not to say "Helloooo??!" when she is quiet for too long. That just yields an icy stare. I want to be sure we cover all our needs, requests and praises…and those of our friends and family too. It's a long list and requires quite some time. Val however, seems clueless about the day's schedule. She takes an interminable period of time just to get out the first word of her prayer, 'Father' …and then who knows how long it will be before the next word comes out of her mouth! With all that I have on my plate, it's really hard for me to waste that time with her. But if I actually said that to her, can you imagine the silent treatment I would get?

"Boy, when it comes to our spiritual walk together, she sure can give a whole new set of nuances to the words 'quiet time!'"

Daily Devotionals: Daily Devotionals Together

Day One:

1. <u>Bible Reading</u>: In Luke 5 we read: "Yet the news about him spread all the more, so that crowds of people came to hear him and to be healed of their sicknesses. But Jesus often withdrew to lonely places and prayed." Luke 5: 15-16

   Often times we use the excuses of "not often time" or "too much to do" to justify not spending a devotional time together. When demands increased on Jesus, what did he do? How often do you think "often" needs to be for you and your spouse to have effective devotional time together?

2. <u>Journal Time</u>: Record any decisions you made about "how often" and "how much time" you are going to dedicate to developing the devotional aspect of your marriage.

3. <u>Prayer Time</u>: Ask God to help you protect the time you devote to pursuing the devotional/spiritual side of your relationship together.

Day Two:
1. <u>Bible Reading</u>: Today we are going to look at the same verse we did yesterday, Luke 5:15-16: "Yet the news about him spread all the more, so that crowds of people came to hear him and to be healed of their sicknesses. But Jesus often withdrew to lonely places and prayed." Luke 5: 15-16

a. List some of the benefits Jesus must have gained as a result of spending this time with His Heavenly Father.

b. Are those same benefits available to us as individuals? As couples? Can what you receive as an individual be shared as a couple? Explain your answers.

2. Journal Time: Record the blessings/benefits of spending time with God.

3. Prayer Time: Thank God for the benefits you have received as a result of spending time with Him. If you haven't experienced them yet, thank Him in advance for what you trust Him to do as you spend time together with Him.

Day Three:
1. Bible Reading: Psalms 1:1-3 says, "Blessed is the one who does not walk in step with the wicked or stand in the way that sinners take or sit in the company of mockers, but whose delight is in the law of the LORD, and who meditates on his law day and night. That person is like a tree planted by streams of water, which yields its fruit in season and whose leaf does not wither—whatever they do prospers." Psalms 1:1-3
    a. What does it mean to meditate on God's Word "day and night"?

b. What are the helpful warnings and blessings that come from meditating on and living out the truths of God's Word?

2. <u>Journal Time</u>: Make a list of some of the ways God has warned and/or blessed you. Write as if you were leaving this list for your heirs to read someday.

3. <u>Prayer Time</u>: Thank God for the blessings He has already given you as a result of following Him and the truths of His Word. Pray about the needs you and your family have. Ask God to give you opportunities to share with family some stories of how God has blessed you.

Day Four:

1. <u>Bible Reading</u>: In the Gospel of Mark we read a passage similar in content to what we shared in Luke 5. Mark 1 reads: "Very early in the morning, while it was still dark, Jesus got up, left the house and went off to a solitary place, where he prayed. Simon and his companions went to look for him, and when they found him, they exclaimed: "Everyone is looking for you!" Jesus replied, "Let us go somewhere else—to the nearby villages—so I can preach there also. That is why I have come." So he traveled throughout Galilee, preaching in their synagogues and driving out demons." Mark 1:35-39

a. In these verses we read of Jesus "escaping" the demands of the day to be with God. When His disciples went looking for him and then found him, what was on their mind? What do you think was on Jesus' mind?

b. Do you see a connection between the time Jesus spent in prayer that day and what He went on to do that day? What might be the lesson for couples especially if/when they have a demanding day ahead of them?

2. Journal Time: What do you think are some of the most demanding areas of your marriage these days? List them as an act of prayer.

3. Prayer Time: You may be in a demanding day, week or season. Ask God to empower you both to positively face the day. If you are in a great season of rest and peace, pray for those who aren't.

Day Five:
1. Bible Reading: In Joshua chapter 24 we read: "…if serving the LORD seems undesirable to you, then choose for yourselves this day whom you will serve, whether the gods your ancestors served beyond the Euphrates, or the gods of the Amorites, in whose land you are living. But as for me and my household, we will serve the LORD." Joshua 24:15 (NIV)
    a. What clear indicators are there to show that you and your family do indeed serve the Lord? How might you incorporate a daily devotional for your whole family (no matter where they live) to model/demonstrate your service/availability to the Lord?

    b. If you still have children at home, research some devotional aids for families…and determine to use them.

("Keys for Kids" is one such resource). If you are an empty nester.... how might you encourage your children, nieces, nephews to have devotional times with their spouse?

2. Journal Time: Record the names of your children and grandchildren or nieces/nephews asking God to help them establish a daily time with God as individuals, couples, and/or families. Use this list as a reminder to pray for them daily together as a couple.

3. Prayer Time: Pray for any children that aren't walking with the Lord these days. Pray for those that are following Jesus and are married to begin having devotional times together if they aren't doing so already.

Chapter Five
Romance

Determined!

Life had become, well, so "daily" for Terry and Corinne. Their dating years had been good. Actually dating "months" would be more accurate; so genuine, passionate, "fast and furious" was their love and romance. However, as is so often the case with couples, careers took off, kids came along, as many kids and more than they had hoped for; six to be exact, ranging in age from four to fourteen. Managing a family this size required a solid schedule. Skillfully, Terry and Corinne had cobbled together a dependable yet fast-paced routine where each played their multi-faceted roles.

There was the never-ending "homemaker work shift" and all it entailed for Corinne. Her work included being the family: chauffer, cook, counselor, comforter, clothier, nurse, maid/housekeeper, launderer, gardener, tutor, keeper of the social calendar and, oh yes, wife. (If you were to determine the hourly wage for each role and the numbers of hours she spent at each role, her financial contribution to the family was substantial.) Corinne had so much ability and education. But she gave up her career as a respiratory therapist to stay home with the kids. It was a huge sacrifice for Terry and Corinne…but so worth it! For instance, she did indeed get to see almost all of their children's "firsts".

For Terry, there was the corporate eight a.m. to five p.m. shift. He was the primary bread winner. But his work didn't stop when he left his office. There were always calls to make, orders to fill, paper work to be done and complaints to be handled well after he had left the business complex. On top of all that he was the family: sports coach, advisor, fight-settler, carpenter, plumber, electrician, roofer, gymnastic apparatus (the kids loved to climb on and wrestle with him), vacation planner, accountant, spiritual head-of-the-home and, oh yes, husband. (His "hourly" rates and total could also be figured as "substantial.")

Together, they had their schedule logically worked out: soccer, ballet, church, youth group, trade club, golf, fishing, quilting, school, yard work, house work, "work work" …not necessarily in that order. But by the grace of God they were able to establish and manage a routine that functioned like a fine Swiss watch.

Routine? Well "yes," that described their family life and now hauntingly, their romance. Had they become too predictable with each other? Was there still passion in their marriage? Were their kisses and hugs too routine and too predictable? (Like when Terry leaves for or comes home from work?) There used to be such trusting mystery with each other; some might call it a "spark." Did that spark and mystery have to be sacrificed merely because they were getting older and they had such a big family? These questions wheeled in their minds like condors over carrion. Was something "dead" in their relationship? If so, could it be revived? Alone, in a rare just-the-two-them over dinner moment they shared an idea. It sounded something like this: "We used to be so passionate. What if we rekindled the romance in our marriage?! How would we do that?" The conversation quickly moved from "What if?" to "Let's do this!" They were determined to be romantic, again! Simultaneously they thought, "This is awesome!" (Good for us!!!) Their ensuing strategy was to each plan a separate, surprise, romantic weekend getaway. It would be carried out somewhere in the next six months. With cheer-leader-like enthusiasm, Corinne shouted louder than even she expected, "This is going to be epic!"

They agreed to a couple simple rules so as not to foul things up from the start. Rule number one: Terry would go first. After all, they didn't want to <u>really</u> surprise each other by both planning a romantic getaway on the same weekend. Rule number two: They had to incorporate all five senses into their plan (sight, sound, smell, taste, and touch).

So, going first, even though he felt rushed, Terry went "planning away" as only he could. To himself he mused, "If only I had more time, I could really get this right." But forced ahead by his own expectations, he laid out a strategy.

Here's what Terry planned for Corinne…

He had a friend who owned an isolated mansion in the nearby foothills of the Sierra Nevada mountains. It's location and availability fit perfectly into Terry's concept of a great romantic getaway.

To get to the mansion, they would have to drive about 45 minutes across the valley and into the foothills. At the correct point on the highway, they would take a right turn, off the main highway, having just passed the sign that indicated a national park was a few miles ahead. Having taken that right turn, a short drive would bring them to a locked gate. Once passed the gate a long, graveled, uphill road would eventually deliver them to the front entrance of the stately mansion. It was royally situated on a hill overlooking the lake on the other side of the main road. (If they turned left instead of right off the main highway, they would end up at the lake's main boat ramp.) The owner had moved to another state, so the house was on the market but currently empty. Terry saw this as a "plus" and was able to "furnish" it with just the right accouterments for their perfect get away: a microwave oven, a portable stereo, a DVD player and accompanying flat-screen, an air mattress, a small table, two folding chairs and some disposable eating utensils and of course a coffee maker. He, being logical, knew women were stereotypically emotional, so he had also rented some "better have a Kleenex box handy" movies. He reasoned, "Tugging at her heart strings would get her in the right mood."

At this point in his planning, everything was going better than he had expected. Secretly transporting the furniture in his truck to the mansion proved to be easier than he first thought. When it came to the menu for the weekend, the first night's dinner was an easy choice for him. But he wondered, "How am I going to sufficiently refrigerate the perishables, so they'll last the entire weekend? Again, he talked to himself. "Ah, get a large ice chest like the one's on TV that are rated for multiple days. For good measure, I'll add a chunk of dry ice. I can get dry ice at the grocery store. Or maybe I'll park our RV in front of the mansion (it had a nice refrigerator). Nah, that's overkill, stick with the ice chest." Terry was indeed getting lost in the weekend's details. When he finally settled on a good refrigeration plan, he started going through their five-senses list.

Here's some of the trails surprisingly taken by his near-dormant creative side:

Sight?: To himself he thought, "I have that one covered in spades! How could I find a more beautiful setting than that? The hilltop view of the lake is spectacular and the sunsets even more so up there. I hope she wasn't thinking "sight" included me. I weigh too much these days."

Sound?: Hmmm…this one was going to be a little more difficult. He remembered that years ago she liked saxophone music. Wondering out loud he said, "Does she still like it? Is Kenny G still making romantic CDs? Should I make my own selection of romantic songs? What will happen if a song plays that reminds her of a former boyfriend? Maybe I should ask her…but where's the surprise in that? I should probably do some research on the internet and/or via her friends. How does sound factor in when we go to bed for the night? Will my snoring be considered a 'minus' in the 'sound' category?" Boy, he discovered this piece of the puzzle was going to take a lot of research and some serious analytical self-talk; much more than his not-so-creative brain and jittery nerves were offering him now.

Smell?: Terry thought to himself, "Apple scented candles? Or would that just make her hungry? (He seemed to recall she was trying to lose some weight.) Don't I have some cologne somewhere…. a Father's Day gift from years back? How long does cologne 'keep'? How would I know if it has gone bad? Could I get a rash from it or even worse give one to her?" His mind was wandering now so he reined it back in in.

Taste?: His thinking continued: "Well, there is the first night's meal which consists of rice pilaf, lamb shish kabobs from my favorite Greek restaurant, a big loaf of French bread, sweet tea, and chocolate cake. Will she want a salad? Will she want dressing? And what will we eat for the rest of the weekend? How 'bout anything that ends with "o's": Cheerios, Fritos, Doritos, taquitos, burritos, Oreos. Nice! I can empty and reuse several of the medium-sized moving boxes I saw in the garage. I'll pack them with scads of easy-to-eat food and snacks. This meal prep is going to be easier than I thought. The great food and glorious location I secured for us has got to yield a great romantic weekend," he reasoned to no one in particular. "Corinne is going to be so impressed. I'll even include those green-foil-wrapped after-dinner mints she likes so much."

Touch?: Terry chuckled as he thought, "Duh, if we aren't touching each other how could it possibly be a romantic getaway? Piece o' cake! She won't be able to keep her hands off of me when she sees all I have done for her!"

Finally, after all his prep work, the special weekend rolled around. Proud as a peacock, confident in his plan, he revealed to Corinne that this was the surprise romantic weekend. The kids were cooperating with the grandparents who had come for the weekend. The car was packed and ready to roll. Corinne wondered how in the world he pulled all this together without her noticing a thing. But she excused herself by recalling, she had been pre-occupied with "winning" via her supermom jam-packed routine. And she had to give herself some slack due to her time-consuming preoccupation with new recipes which of course required a whole new healthy-eating grocery list. Anyway, she broke from these nano-second-long mental rabbit trails, re-entered the family circus of "instructions, hugs, and goodbyes," grabbed a few last-minute things, then out the door and down the driveway they rolled. Terry had even managed to wash and vacuum their car.

Terry was sharing intimate thoughts with Corinne when, not too far from home, he stopped at a drive-thru restaurant, got out, walked around to her side of the car, opened her door and started acting like this was the location for their first night's special dinner. (What a great plan he had! His confidence was soaring, so he was feeling quite playful this first night.) When she hesitantly started to get out, he stopped her, kissed her on the forehead and said, "Just kidding." He closed the door, walked back to his side, got in and away they drove to another drive-thru where another "tease" was repeated. Terry was amused. Corinne was too, the first time, but not so much the second and third times. She thought to herself, "Enough already, we're wasting time. Let's get to the adventuresome parts while I still have strength!"

Terry finally pointed their car towards their hilltop hideaway. When he arrived at the dirt road turn-off, leaving the main highway, he only needed to travel a short distance before he stopped the car. He got out, walked to the locked end of the gate, unlocked it, then swung it out of the way. He got back in the car, kissed Corinne then drove passed the gate. Once on the other side, he got out again, smiled in anticipation at Corinne, swung the gate closed, locked it, re-entered the car, then drove up the long winding gravel road to the hill-top mansion. Corinne was getting a bit impatient with all this "pomp and circumstance" over unlocking then re-locking the gate, yet from deep within her soul, she also felt a growing sense of excitement. Her inner voice said, "Now we are getting to the good parts. I just love adventure! I wonder what amazing excursions he has planned up here?" When they parked in front of the mansion, Corinne was really impressed with its regal beauty. To top it off the sun was about an hour from setting; a spectacular, this-day-only vista was starting to form.

"Are we going on a hike, now? Will we ride quads to the higher peaks? Are we going to the lake across the highway for a sunset cruise on the water?" Inside her mind Corinne was caught up with the challenging possibilities. Instead they went inside for dinner. She did her best to hide her mild disappointment. Once they familiarized themselves with the locations of the mansions' rooms and light switches, they both simultaneously realized they were quite hungry. Maybe their hunger was due in part to seeing several fast-food marquises earlier that evening? Terry responded to their growling stomachs by portioning their respective meals on paper plates. The food was now ready for the microwave. If Terry was anything he was "practical."

As the food heated up, the smell of garlic filled the room. Terry loved it. Corinne wondered about them kissing with "garlic mouth." (Subconsciously, critically she reasoned, "This is not what I had in mind for the 'smell' and 'taste' categories.") Just then, she noticed music starting to cue up from the adjacent living room. "Am I hearing saxophone music? Isn't that a bit cliché?" she thought. "And besides whoever that sax player is, he doesn't have the 'touch' my former favorite saxophonist had. Oh well, at least Terry is trying."

When dinner was done (way too much starch and not enough vegetables for her) dessert was presented and boy was it good. Chocolate cake! Her favorite! Was there no coffee to go with it?

They danced, or due to lack of lessons, merely shuffled around to Mr. "not that good of a sax player." It was romantic to be in each other's embrace and to see the sun starting to set through the massive windows that spanned the western side of the living room. ("Too late for any out of doors activities; opportunity missed," she opined in her mind.)

When the saxophone CD stopped, Terry dashed to start the DVD; his plan called for no break in their romantic mood. Everything was going so well, it was hard for him to hide his smile. "You've Got Mail" featuring Tom Hanks and Meg Ryan was introduced on the flat screen he had hauled up the hill. In her mind Corinne mumbled, "We have seen this way too many times." Terry thought he sensed a lack of enthusiasm on her part. But because it didn't fit with his preconceptions about the movies' romantic impact, he quickly, subconsciously dismissed her non-verbal cue.

They snuggled up on the air-bed as best they could. It was under inflated making them feel more like parallel hot dogs in a gigantic bun. They hadn't used it in so long neither one knew it had a hole in it, somewhere. Oh well, fortunately it was a slow leak.

They settled in for the movie and time rolled by. By the time Tom, Meg and Brinkley-the-dog met in the flower-spangled park scene, Terry and Corinne were nearly asleep. He had expected some love making at the end of the evening. She had expected an adventure and maybe some love making afterwards. Neither had expected to fall asleep before the movie mercifully ended. As the sound of sleep-induced heavy breathing filled the room, the flat screen went "dormant" for the night.

The following morning, Corinne woke up before the sun did. Terry slept until eight. From her perspective the best part of the day, morning, was nearly gone; wasted. From his perspective, the rest was fantastic and much needed.

When coffee beans danced inside the grinder, Terry inter-preted the noise as his wakeup call. As the beans submitted to the grinders' fast-moving blades, the rattle of their grinder-dance turned into more of a purr. The sound echoed throughout the empty mansion. Prompted by the sound of the coffee mill, Terry nearly got out of bed but instead rolled over on his side and was almost asleep again. Head on pillow and eyes still closed, a smile began to form on his face. The smile was prompted by the pleasant aroma emanating from the brewing of his favorite dark roast coffee. The fragrance seemed to fill the whole house. As part of her usual morning routine, Corinne had ground the beans then loaded and started the coffee maker; she just couldn't wait anymore to see if Terry was going to perform today's barista duties.

"Hey, you're doing my job!" That reality had suddenly dawned on Terry. Newly inspired to be "romantic", and with a burst of unusual morning energy (a jolt of adrenalin?), he scrambled out of their nearly flat air mattress. His hair was sticking out everywhere in classic bed-head fashion. He was barely dressed but had quickly put on his black leather slip-ons to protect his feet from the cold tile floors; he was quite the site. And "oh my!" talk about bad breath! Dragons would be no match for the garlic-laced vapor that issued from his mouth. In spite of his un-romantic appearance and smell, he was determined to add something pleasing to the morning meal. He opened the top box of his stack of medium sized cardboard moving boxes. It, like the other two boxes in the stack was packed with the treasure trove of "O's".

Terry was pleased as punch.

Corinne was "bummed" at the mere site of the waist expanding caloric extravaganza.

And that's when she just couldn't contain her disappointment anymore. Near tears, arms limp at her sides, head down and shoulders slumping she whimpered, "Can we just go home?" She tried to express her gratitude for his effort but she just couldn't do this anymore. There wasn't enough reserve energy in her. Terry gave her an understanding hug, but still, he was crushed. He thought to himself, "All this work, energy, effort and money! I mean, I even addressed all five senses yet apparently somehow still so misread her romantic expectations?"

As they packed up then headed home, both were wondering, "Is romance dead in our marriage? Does it have to die?" They weren't sure. They hoped it wasn't so. But Terry was comforted by the knowledge that hidden in the secret calendar of Corinne's mind were still the dates of her romantic getaway-plan custom designed for Terry. She was comforted by the knowledge that she could quite easily surpass Terry's romantic efforts. When Terry said something, which Corinne interpreted as agreement with her private but unmentioned better-at-romance thoughts, Corinne's response helped him, better "them" hang on to hope; but they didn't have near as much hope as when this experiment began.

Would they try this again? Yes, they simply had to (must?) rekindle their romance. The proverbial ball was now in Corinne's court and she was exceedingly confident she could do much better than Terry.

She, (or was it really "they"?) was determined to be romantic!

Couples Daily Devotionals: Romance

Day One:

1. <u>Bible Reading</u>: Song of Solomon 4:1-7 and 5:10-18. Do you
    think your spouse would respond well to a word-for-word
    description from these verses? Maybe not. So how might
    you speak to your spouse in a way that would please
    him/her? Wife/husband, how would you like your spouse to
    romantically communicate with you? What are some
    listening skills you may need to improve to better
    communicate with each other?

2. <u>Journal Time</u>: Record your findings from the Bible Reading
    discussion questions.

3. <u>Prayer Time</u>: Pray that you will discover (or re-discover) the
    romance that is most appropriate for you and your spouse and
    that it will truly satisfy both your souls.

Day Two:
1. <u>Bible Reading</u>: Song of Solomon 1:1-16. Today, when
    you read this chapter, take note of how many of the five
    human senses are employed in their romance. What are
    some ways you could follow their example?

2. <u>Journal Time</u>: Record your answers from the Bible Reading discussion questions.

3. <u>Prayer Time</u>: Pray that God will increasingly give you the willingness and trust to be vulnerable to each other as you express your romantic hopes. Pray also for the courage to act on your romance discussions.

Day Three:

1. <u>Bible Reading</u>: Read Hebrews 13:4. What do you think "keep the marriage bed pure" means? In Christian marriage, how do you balance purity and the married couples' freedom to enjoy sex?

2. <u>Journal Time</u>: What would be some guidelines you can agree on for keeping "pure" the sexual elements of your marriage? Adventuresome?

3. <u>Prayer Time</u>: Ask God to help you remain sexually pure yet romantically involved with each other.

Day Four:

1. <u>Bible Reading</u>: Read Genesis 2:25. Adam and Eve felt no shame about being naked with each other. What does this say about them physically, emotionally, spiritually? Are there physical, emotional, spiritual elements of your marriage where you <u>do</u> feel shame? What might be a good plan to help move from shame to celebration?

   On a spiritual level: Do you feel totally accepted by God? What evidence might you give that demonstrates you do or don't feel totally accepted by God? Do you feel totally accepted by your spouse? What evidence might you give that demonstrates you do or don't feel totally accepted by your spouse?

2. <u>Journal Time</u>: Record your answers (goals?) derived from your answers to the Bible Reading questions.

3. <u>Prayer Time</u>: Ask God to help you conquer any issues of fear or shame related to the romantic aspect of your life together.

Day Five:

1. <u>Bible Reading</u>: Read Psalms 139:14. God designed and made us according to His good purposes. This implies he also created sex and he created the way each individual best perceives romance. Romance involves more than just sex. Discuss with each other how you feel about God creating sex. Discuss with each other what "romance" means and/or implies to you. Do you feel emotionally connected to each other? What are your expectations?

2. <u>Journal Time</u>: Record your plan to surprise your spouse with a romantic getaway according to your spouses' needs. Share with each other what you hope will occur at this getaway. Record who first plans and carries out this retreat. Agree to a time frame for going on this getaway, for example: "Somewhere in the next 3 months I'll plan one, then you plan the next one before the next 3 months pass, ok?"

3. <u>Prayer Time</u>: Ask God to help you with your attitudes about romance and your plans to be more romantic.

Chapter Six
What About the Inside of the Cup?

Where Did __That__ Come From?

Tom and Lynn had been married for 156 months. At least that was the way they measured the time invested in their marriage. Their reasoning? They felt strongly that they should celebrate their wonderful union "monthly" instead of just annually. If the curious pressed them for years their typical answer at this point was "about thirteen." They had made good use of their thirteen years getting to know each other than starting a family.

Tom was excited to have a big family. His family of origin had nine children. Lynn was not as enthusiastic about having nine children, so they agreed on four biological children with the possibility of adoption after that. Child number four was already on the way. Maybe they might adopt twins after he or she arrived.

Their three elementary age children couldn't wait for this fourth child to come from mommy's burgeoning tummy. They really wanted to play with him or her; they didn't care which. (Tom and Lynn had decided not to discover the baby's gender until the day of its birth.) However, the arrival date was still two months away which seemed like forever in a child's mind.

On this particular summer day, Tom woke up to the usual raucous laughter of his kids playing. They had built a "fort" out of the larger pillows scavenged from every piece of furniture in the house. The smaller pillows they amassed were being used for hand-to-hand combat and as missiles in imagined dire emergencies. Nothing had been broken, yet. But the possibility of damage increased as the kids became more and more rambunctious.

Moving along nicely in his get-to-the-office morning routine, Tom put his shoes on as the finishing touch of today's business ensemble. He grabbed his brief case before heading down the hallway to the kitchen. There he scarfed down his cereal, grabbed a power-drink, waded into the sea of scattered pillows, then kissed each of the kids goodbye. He knew time was escaping him, so he hurriedly headed for the front door of their nice three-and-two.

As he dodged one last pillow/missile, a near miss by one of the older kids, Lynn grabbed him by his tie, swept her bedraggled hair back over her ears, then kissed him one more time before he walked out the front door. "I love you," Lynn reminded him. "I love you too. Wish I didn't have to go to work," was Tom's heartfelt reply. And with that he stepped out into the world beyond their front door.

Yet, once outside he lingered, lured by the happy sounds from inside the house. His hand still on the outer door knob, Tom could hear the kids' loud laughter. He thought, "They are really ramping up today." He was sad and glad at the same time that he had escaped the chaos of the kids.

Lynn was glad he closed the front door quickly. It was hot and humid outside. "Best to keep that outside," she thought. It would be inhumane to ask the kids to play in this heat, unless their portable pool was already inflated and filled. No matter how much the kids begged her, she just didn't have the energy to brave the heat of the storage shed where the pool was kept. She just didn't have the energy for such a humanitarian task because building a human being inside her own body was exhausting enough. To herself she thought, "Too bad they didn't think of that aquatic activity before Tom bolted."

Lynn's stomach was now roaring like a lion giving his kingdom "notice." Yes, she knew she was eating for two, but at times the intensity of her hunger surprised even her. Her mood would best be described as ravenously hungry with a dash of crankiness.

Even louder than the roar of her stomach was the sound of the kids' battle. And as is the case in all "warfare," at some point in time the troops must be fed. Their fort-building, castle-storming, missile-launching, pillow-fighting and various other random imaginary situations that required their immediate action at any given moment, caused a considerable calorie burn. As soon as Lynn started rummaging through the cupboards, the kids in seeming synchronization all heard the familiar sound associated with feeding time. While their bodies remained frozen in whatever contorted position the moment found them, their heads simultaneously pivoted to focus on Lynn's dutiful search. She was hoping to find anything to satisfy her current craving for something savory. The kids had other food thoughts. She noticed it had become quite quiet, so without letting go of the cupboard handle, she peered over her shoulder only to see them all staring at her.

"Mommy," with all the drama of a Charles Dickens street urchin, one of them whined, "Please may we have some pancakes?" The others chimed in and someone said, "Sausage too!?" Suddenly it was as if her name was "Flo" and their home mysteriously transformed from a battle zone to a road side café. To herself she accommodatingly thought: "Moms were supposed to be busboys (set the table), waitresses (take the individual orders), short order cooks (cook great food fast) and dishwashers (obvious) all rolled into one, right?" She started inventorying what pancake ingredients were available. While surveying her cupboards, she had simultaneously assembled a saltine slathered with peanut butter and topped with a pickle chip plus one thick slice of smoked summer sausage. Her mouth was already watering. She opened wide then delicately placed the whole cracker onto her waiting tongue. When her lips came back together, having closed her mouth and her eyes, she savored the satisfying combination of flavors. To her it was like a culinary rest stop in "heaven." Moving quickly, she prepared a second saltine. She covered this one with a whole spoonful of crunchy style peanut butter. At this very instant, it was hovering over her tongue. Before she could set it on her tongue, one of the kids launched a pillow-missile that knocked the saltine out of her fingers. It ricocheted off her wrist then amazingly affixed itself to the side of her face. Though a random act, the square cracker was placed as if by the skill of a tile setter. The kids howled at the landing of this "one in a million" shot. "Funny, but not cool," she thought. She deftly pried the cracker off her cheek while giving the kids a mock menacing smile. Then with a flick of her wrist she popped the whole cracker in her mouth. In her calmest parental voice, she said, "Be careful kids!" It was about all her remaining patience could think to say at this low blood sugar moment. She had benignly decided to accommodate their behavior rather than rebuke it. Besides the "cracker on the cheek" shot was funny, really.

It was still way too early a morning for her. But she forced her mind to re-start analyzing her breakfast situation. She also had hopes of coming up with some safe, fun summer time activities for her and the kids. She really did want them to have fun. After all, weren't she and Tom the ones that taught the kids to build pillow forts? She had to come up with some new adventures that would engage them yet keep them from being punished for being, well, kids. What could she come up with that would neither bore them nor burden her less than adequate energy reserves? She was deep in thought about the possibilities, but her food craving maw caused her to re-focus.

Lynn managed to cobble together the right ingredients for some kind of low-budget pancake. The batter was mixed and now patiently awaiting the griddle's amber "ready" indicator light to cycle on. It seemed like forever before it finally did cycle on thus signaling, "Pour the batter now!" The moment she started pouring, and at nearly the same moment another "pillow bazooka" misfired, sending the errant "round" straight for the plastic bowl that contained the pancake batter. "Unbelievable!" It was a second one in a million shot! It sent pancake batter spraying 180 degrees and somewhat more. The ceiling was covered. The counter was covered. The floor was covered. The refrigerator behind her was covered. The backsplash behind the cookie jar was covered. (How could it possibly get behind the cookie jar that was below a counter top cabinet?) She didn't have her glasses on yet, thank God, but her vision was unusually blurred by her batter-basted bangs that momentarily held, then released the slow-moving goo. Without moving a muscle, trying to maintain her composure, she let it continue down her forehead, down the bridge of her nose, over her lips, finally dripping off her chin. Her face, pajamas and favorite furry pink slippers were covered with room temperature, off white stucco. The kids were laughing their heads off. She felt like cutting their heads off.

From somewhere deep inside her, an emotional lava flow was making its way to the surface. She felt it rising. She knew her mouth was about to "vent" a pyroclastic flow. Sulfuric acid-laced steam was about to spew. Inside her soul, wave after wave of pent up frustration, hurt, sadness, and disappointment, (some that had nothing to do with her children) started merging and growing from smaller to larger streams. To use another analogy, her negative and painful memories combined like rocket fuel with the hormonal cocktail of a woman in her third trimester of pregnancy. When she recalled some TV psychologist's advice to let her anger out, the moment of ignition arrived. Her recall of his tempting voice was all the prompt she needed: she blew her top. Spectacular screaming as effective as a cyclone warning siren issued from her mouth. Her arms were moving to effectively give gesture to her words, but they were moving so fast it was difficult to determine what gesture went with which words. There was a vein popping out on her reddened forehead and one on each side of her neck. Her eyes were wide and seemed to never even blink. In all, Vesuvius's explosion barely surpassed hers. The pyrotechnic outburst was spectacular by any measurement, unless one was on the receiving end or was measuring healthy relationships.

Her words continued to fly out of her mouth with the staccato bursts of a volcano-sized Roman candle. Verbal smoke and ash seemed to be everywhere. To save their lives, the kids exaggerated, they dove under the kitchen table or the pillow fort, whichever was closer. They had rarely seen such a fiery display from mom.

About mid-explosion, her cell phone started vibrating. For some strange reason, she actually stopped yelling long enough to see who was calling. It was the Director of Women's Ministries from their church. (Lynn was a revered Bible teacher for the main sessions of their Wednesday morning studies.) Mercifully for the kids, Lynn answered the call with the sweetest voice one could imagine. Angels would have been proud of the graceful words that flowed from her lips as she and the director exchanged pleasantries then information about the upcoming young mothers' community outreach. The topic Lynn was to present was "Being in Touch with your Emotions."

Eventually their discussion wound down and ended with an over-the-phone prayer offered by the Director. Lynn agreed with the prayer, offering her non-verbal approvals and occasional "amens" until their last amen mutually ended the prayer.

As she cleaned up the pancake batter, and the kids re-emerged from their hiding places like timid fawns testing the meadow after their first encounter with summer thunder, Lynn wondered to herself, "Where did that come from? And how in the world could I so dramatically change my behavior when the Director called? How would I possibly describe this to Tom? Would the kids get to him first? If so, what would their version be? What did that outburst reveal about what is really going on in my soul? How much more 'soul work' do I need?"

Couples' Daily Devotionals: Where Did That Come From?

Day One:

1. <u>Bible Reading</u>: Read I John 4:18.
   a. Why are couples afraid to deal with what is "inside the cup". Is that true for you? Your spouse? Why?

   b. Express your love and total acceptance of your spouse, faults and all....and a willingness to seek out help for any faults that need God-honoring change.

2. <u>Journal Time</u>: Record any fears of disclosure you may have. Cast them out! Make a commitment today to no longer let any kind of unhealthy fear rule in your individual lives or your marriage.

3. <u>Prayer Time</u>: Read Jeremiah 31:3b then pray together asking God to help you understand how much you each other and how perfectly you are loved by God.

Day Two:

1. <u>Bible Reading</u>: Psalms 103:13-14 and Psalms 139: 1-3. Since God knows you completely, including what is in your heart, does it make sense to try to hide anything from Him? (Cf. Genesis 3:8-9) Wouldn't it be better to invite the Holy

Spirit to help you deal with what is in your heart that is not pleasing to God?

2. Journal Time: What are some issues of the heart that you and/or your spouse need to deal with? Make a list of the issues of the heart that need God's healing touch.

3. Prayer Time: Thank God for knowing us through-and-through, yet still loving us completely. Praise Him for His love and grace. Invite the Holy Spirit in to assist you in any repentance and/or healing of the heart.

Day Three:

1. Bible Reading: Read James 4:1 and James 2:12-13. What does this verse reveal about the fallen nature of our souls? What soul issues do you and/or your spouse struggle with the most? How does that affect your marriage?

2. Journal Time: Record some soul changing ways (as opposed to mere behavior modification) you and your spouse can deal with this fallen nature (issues of the heart).

3. <u>Prayer Time</u>: Ask the Holy Spirit to help you conquer some of the adverse aspects of your souls. And ask Him to empower you to treat each other with great love, respect and honor; as children of the King. Remember, God loves you just the way you are but He loves you too much to leave you that way.

Day Four:

1. <u>Bible Reading</u>: Did you identify with any of Lynn's explosive behavior? If so, according to Matthew 5: 23-24, what should be done with/for the recipients of that behaviour? Be sure to include any appropriate "restitution" in your answer(s).

2. <u>Journal Time</u>: Record any people you might need to be reconciled to.

3. <u>Prayer Time</u>: Ask God to give you opportunity to be reconciled to those who have been the recipient of any of your un-Christlike behavior. You might also ask them to keep praying for you so you don't "act out" again. (Note: If you have children, you might want to ask them if you ever done anything that offended them and now still bothers them. What a great time for reconciliation!)

Day Five:

1. <u>Bible Reading</u>: Proverbs 20:5 says, "The purposes of a person's heart are deep waters, but one who has insight draws them out." If what is in your soul is hard for

you to identify, who might be a source of help? Hint: How is God's activity or character described in John 14:26 and Isaiah 9:6?

2. Journal Time: What might be some issues-of-the-heart you would like to deal with? Make a commitment to talk with and pray with each other over these issues.

3. Prayer Time: Ask the Holy Spirit to help you better understand why you and your spouse act the way you do. Ask God to help you improve the good things you do and to gain victory over the bad things you do.

Chapter Seven
Spiritual Gifting(s) and Us

Bob knew he was called to be a pastor; well, he was fairly certain about that. He had heard his own pastor say, "If you can do anything else and be happy, you are probably not 'called.'" Bob saw the wisdom in that statement. He knew he was called but didn't want to be. From his family's church experience, he knew how pastors were too often treated poorly. Besides, his fun-loving personality was ill-suited to being a pastor, or so he thought. Growing up in the church, most pastors he knew were rather serious most of the time. He definitely did not fit that mold.

When Bob couldn't get into dental or medical school, still not giving up that dream, as an intermediary step he had become a laboratory technologist. He was an outstanding Tech at three different medical facilities by the time he was 28. He was at the last independent lab for six years but soon realized the owners' business plan and leadership skills were woefully inadequate. After all this private lab was run by pathologists not trained businessmen. A dead-end job was all Bob could strategically envision here. A growing family and the expenses that go with it pretty much put an end to the dream of having his own dental or medical practice.

Not happy and restless of soul, Bob decided to buy a restaurant franchise along with two fellow investors who were close friends. But interest rates skyrocketed at the same time. The fledgling partnership knew their venture was stillborn.

Next came a stint with an insurance company. Here was a chance for Bob to strategically plan, act quickly, advance and conquer... all the while efficiently providing a great income for his still growing family. Of course, a tenth of all the promised money would be given to boost the work of God's Kingdom. (Bob liked to comfort his soul with that last thought.) The insurance job did work. He was blessed. Money rolled in, but deep within the recesses of his heart he was pretty sure he was running from God's call on his life. Bob still wasn't happy.

After much financial success but misery of soul he finally decided to tell Diane, "I think I am supposed to be a pastor." When they started dating she had voiced her hope to be a pastor's wife. Bob made it quite clear to her that that would never happen. However, she could see God's call on his life via the fruit born whenever he carried out some of the roles of pastoring in their local church. For years on end she had prayed that he would someday soon say "yes" to God's call. After all, she reasoned, I don't want to be married to a "Jonah."

Then one holiday season it happened. In a burning bush-like moment, Bob felt that God was speaking to his heart saying, "Bob, you are at a crossroads. Here's your choice: continue saying 'no' to Me and be miserable the rest of your life OR say 'yes' to me and watch Me bless you, your family and the ministry I will entrust to you." Bob knew that God was enjoying making a tough choice not that tough after all.

In a matter of days, Bob notified his boss of his plans to leave the company. The boss was quite offended at this news. (The boss had invested a lot in Bob. He had also regularly publicly praised Bob as a perfect example; one to be followed.)

In a matter of weeks, they moved one hundred miles to go to seminary, kids and all.

Bob advanced through the curriculum rapidly. God provided for their physical needs adequately. It seemed like just a matter of months, and they were done with school and on to their first church. Graduation and placement had occurred smoothly.

Their five-year tenure at their first church fit the stats nicely; an average stay with results about the same. They parted ways quite in love with most of the congregation but not as much with the board. The board didn't seem to really appreciate all his giftings and abilities. Now, Bob and Diane were ready to move on, in part so they could get away from the "this is just your first church" stigma.

When a different church in a different state opened up, they thought this might be the proverbial ticket. They interviewed and subsequently answered what they believed to be God's call to be the lead pastor. This move to a new church, average in attendance with an almost equally average budget, gave them a wonderful opportunity to start over. They hoped they had learned enough from their first church to have greater effectiveness at their second church.

When they were candidating, the church leadership reminisced about their previous pastor who was such a wonderful shepherd. They were nearly unanimous in their recollection that he "never missed a birthday, anniversary, or hospital visit." Bob wondered if he could possibly fill such big "shepherding shoes." He reasoned, though, that his strategic planning skills, and decisive leadership would yield such a bounty of spiritual and financial fruit that everyone would see the wisdom of having called him. Besides, he did have shepherding skills, they apparently just weren't as dominant as his predecessor's. And once they met the "Diane" part of this duo, they would know that she more than made up for any perceived lack of personal caring by him.

Their "honeymoon" period at the church lasted for the typical period of months. Bob was in rare form energized by this fresh start. He gave his best sermons, complete with Greek and Hebrew verbs parsed to perfection. Biblical archaeology was brought into each message complete with the latest and most colorful version of PowerPoint. His humor shone through too! (People commented how much they appreciated his ability to make learning fun.) The message outlines and small group questions on the flip side of the bulletin insert were, well, "brilliant" in Bob's estimation. The outlines were supported with reference verses and fascinating minutia. The small group questions were clear and provocative. Things were going so well, Bob thought, it was about time they have a combined leadership meeting with all the board members and all leadership volunteers present. That's when things got rough.

Their first vision-planning session was supposed to start at 8:30 one Saturday morning. Bob quickly realized that was not going to happen. At 8:45 even Diane was still out in the hallway sipping coffee and munching on her cinnamon cake-donut as if they all were there for fellowship instead of strategic planning. Only half the leaders were in the room with him; the other half it seemed, were in the hallway with her pondering their myriad donut choices and the latest weather reports. She was supposed to be setting an example by sitting at her duly assigned, perfectly name-plated seat. But no, there she was out in the hallway yucking it up, while directing people to "fill out a name tag and slap it on your chest." Bob was stewing now; he could feel his blood pressure rising. Their delayed start blew his timeline out of the water. Now he was recalculating things like:

- "How do I welcome everyone without taking too much time to do so?" He didn't want to appear to be uncaring at this his first leadership meeting.
- "How can I shorten the starting devotional?" Would doing so make him appear less spiritual?
- "How can I possibly address everything on the agenda?" (He had prayed so hard over that precious agenda.)

In order to get things moving, he decided to step out into the hallway and calmly call everyone to attention. It worked. The other half moved into the room, but their mood had changed from "happy to be here" to "convince me it is worth my time to be here."

Bob moved quickly through the devotional, quicker than he was comfortable with. He asked someone to volunteer to pray over their deliberations. No one volunteered. So, Diane came to the rescue offering prayer for them all. Bob was grateful for her help, but her prayer was too long and off target. He felt she should have been conscious of their late start and kept it short. And no, they weren't "here to get to know each other better," they were here to get things done. He still said "amen" when she did, not so much out of agreement but more for the fact that she was finally done.

Now appropriately blessed and sanctioned by Diane's prayer, Bob got to the real meat of their meeting. His power point presentation was flawless. It was complete with church history, city demographics, attendance and finance charts. Bob had logically and perfectly mapped out where they had been and where they obviously had to go. He was moving through his monologue at a good pace, but their late start obviated the need to cancel the midmorning break. (They had almost started at mid-morning, he imagined.) He unilaterally announced his decision. With no one verbally agreeing or disagreeing, he moved on. They had to move on because he had so much good stuff to discuss!

Well, lunch time rolled around and even though they had covered a lot of ground Bob was mildly unhappy with lack of balance between the remaining agenda and the ever-present, unsympathetic clock ticking away in his brain. He also knew when they returned from lunch some would slip into a post-lunch coma thus curtailing their attentiveness. Competing with that thought was the awareness that, "If we don't break for lunch I might have a mutiny on my hands." Reluctantly, at least in Bob's mind, they stopped for lunch. Bob prayed over the meal, thanking God for His provision and the progress of the morning. Diane bolted for a place in the serving line, grabbed a huge serving spoon and perched herself perfectly to serve from the big aluminum tray of baked beans. She didn't want to miss a single opportunity to meet all the new people brought here by this meeting. She loved blessing every individual with smiles, kind words and yes baked beans concocted from her secret family recipe. Serving each individual brought such fulfillment. She was having a blast!

While he was standing in the food line, a longtime church member and now board member approached Bob asking him to step out of the food line for a moment. Bob was pretty sure of what was coming but felt he really didn't need approval and appreciation just now. He was doing fine, thank you, save the praise for later.

What the man, Carl, told him though was at the same time more and less than what Bob expected. Bob heard something like this:

"We are so glad you are here. We appreciate the strategic aspect you bring to this ministry; we need it. But Bob, I don't know how to say this, so I am just going to spill it out: Are those of us who have faithfully served here for years even needed for your strategy to work? I know that is a blunt thing to say, Bob. But hear me out, please. Did you know that Ron has kept the historical records here for decades? He was shocked that you didn't ask him about his archives...or at least consult with him prior to this meeting. And his wife Jean is usually the one that puts together the PowerPoint presentations. She told me you never even asked her assistance. It's great to see Diane loving on people before the meeting started and now in the serving line. But some of us are wondering if you care about people or are you more concerned about your plans? We are barely taking good care of those who are already here. Now we are wondering who is going to deal with all the new people that might come if your plans pan out. I mean, your heart appears to be more in strategy and advancing the Kingdom via finding the lost...what about caring for the lost and brokenhearted who are already here?" Carl couldn't help but unload the full content of his concern. "In the past, on occasion, some members with the gift of teaching have shared at our main gatherings. Will you now be the only one preaching, teaching and vision-casting? Will you be the only one organizing and administrating? Who will be visiting the newcomers and praying for the sick? Will we still have picnics and potlucks?"

Carl was obviously nervous about sharing all his observations with his new pastor. And when he was finished, Bob wasn't really sure how to respond. So he gave Carl a standard pastor-answer, "Let me pray about this and I'll get back to you Carl. Thank you for being so honest with me. I appreciate it."

Bob was equally nervous about hearing these observations. It significantly upset him, but he knew he couldn't show it. He had now lost his appetite. And he wondered, "Were all these gathered leaders feeling this way? Were there any who were being more realistic and rational like me?"

Again, his calling as a pastor was threatened by some distant recurring voice in his head. (The badgering thought sounded something like, "Maybe you just don't have what it takes!") And his calling to this church was now also in question. To himself Bob reasoned, "Did I misread the high percentage vote? And, if my predecessor was so good and things were so great, why did he leave?" Bob had hoped this would be his second and last church. Now he wasn't quite so sure. He knew everyone had a place in the body of Christ and a "gift" to contribute. He knew he couldn't do it all himself. So, what made them think he was trying to do it all himself?

Well, Bob decided to get back in line and get some of Diane's baked beans after all. He didn't want anyone to sense his surging flood of negative emotions. He sat at a table far from Carl, pushed the beans around his plate, covering well his raw emotions while politely offering some family history to those at his table, when asked. He carefully avoided any topic from the morning's strategic planning session.

The noise of fellowship in the dining hall bounced off the low ceiling. The result was a cacophony of sound that made it challenging to hear people across his table much less his own thoughts. But to himself he was wondering, "Now what do I do? If these people aren't with me, is there any point in covering the rest of this afternoon's agenda? Should I just be transparent with them by sharing what Carl said? What if Carl feels "outed" by me sharing his thoughts? Or maybe worse, what if they all agree with Carl? If these people don't want to advance the Kingdom, were they not honest when I interviewed, or did I merely filter out what I didn't want to hear?" Bob was now nervous, unsure and miserable.

At the same moment, Diane was ecstatic. She was serving the last of her baked beans and connecting with new people like there was no tomorrow. At some point, their eyes met in one of those "across the room syncro-eyes" connections. They had been married long enough for her to pick up the non-verbal cues of Bob's inner turmoil. He subtly motioned to her. When the serving line died down a bit, they stole away for a moment to a quiet hallway. There Bob told her of Carl's comments. In mere seconds, Diane went from smiles to sadness. They couldn't do anything about changing the afternoon's agenda now. They agreed to see it through as planned, but now mere months into their new leadership roles, they were beginning to wonder about coming to this town, this church, these people. Add to it Bob's uncertainty about his calling and gifting… and it's no wonder they were both starting to think, "Are we really needed here or are we simply stuck here?" Stuck here? what a horrible thought and what horrible sounding words they were to this man, this pastor who so wanted to use his gifts to bring God greater glory through advancing His Kingdom.

Couples Daily Devotionals: Spiritual Gifting(s) and Us

Day One:

1. <u>Bible Reading</u>: Read Ephesians 4:7-8
   a. What spiritual gift has God entrusted to you? To your spouse?

      If you don't know what your spiritual gifts are, look up the spiritual gifts assessments available on the internet.

   b. In what ways might you better use these gifts in your marriage? In your extended family? In your church?

   c. What are some healthy ways for people to discover how their spiritual giftings complement each other? Do spiritual gifts ever compete with each other?

2. <u>Journal Time</u>: List the spiritual gifts you believe God has entrusted to you. Also, note the ways God has used those gifts already to bless others.

3. <u>Prayer Time</u>: Pray over and bless your spouse acknowledging the way God has gifted your spouse. Include thanksgiving in your prayer...especially for how your spouses' gifting has blessed you and others.

Day Two:
1. <u>Bible Reading</u>: Read I Corinthians 12: 4-7.

a. Since gifts are given for the "common good", who might benefit from the gift(s) entrusted to you?

b. Lately, have you been using your gift(s) to bless others? Why or why not?

2. <u>Journal Time</u>: What are some opportunities you see where your gifts might be needed? Who do you need to contact to see about using those gifts?

3. <u>Prayer Time</u>: Thank God for the unique way He has gifted you. Ask Him to give you opportunities to use your gifts if you haven't been using them. Also, ask Him to help you grow to be even more effective in the usage of your gifts.

Day Three:
1. <u>Bible Reading</u>: Read I Corinthians 12: 21-26.

a. Have you ever felt like your spiritual gift was not that important? What do these verses teach us about the importance of every gift?

b. Who might try to imply that your gift(s) are unimportant or not needed?

    c.   Do you truly believe that some giftings that are not as visible (public) are as important as those that are? Explain your answer.

    d.   It is sometimes said that "opposites attract". How might this hold true for the spiritual giftings of a couple? How might this hold true for their Strength Deployment Inventory* results?

    e.   Do you have a God-sized dream for your gift's usage or a you-sized dream for its usage? Why?

2.   <u>Journal Time</u>: Record why you think your spiritual gift is "indispensable" to the body of Christ. Also, note a God-sized application of your gift's usage.

3.   <u>Prayer Time</u>: Thank God that before this world began, He already knew you and knew your purpose for being on this planet. (Compare Jeremiah 1:5) Ask Him to help you know the God-sized dreams or plans He has for the usage of the gifts He has entrusted to you.

Day Four:

1.   <u>Bible Reading</u>: Read Ephesians 4:11-13.

    a.   Why were the spiritual gifts given to us?

    b.   According to the last half of verse 13, what is the goal of the usage of our gifts? How do you see this goal being realized through the usage of your gift?

2. Journal Time: Record some ways you and your spouse might together use your spiritual gifts. Be attentive to the ways God might show you opportunities to use your gifts together.

3. Prayer Time: Pray for yourselves and others to become more spiritually mature, more like Christ as a result of you using your spiritual gift(s).

Day Five:

1. Bible Reading: Read Romans 12:3 and I Corinthians 12:7

   a. The spiritual gifts are given for the benefit of others, not to inflate our own egos, right? How might you specifically use your spiritual gift to bless your spouse? Your extended family? The body of Christ?

   b. Do you think God matched you and yours spouse and your spiritual gifts so that you could serve Him together? Do you think God matched you and your spouse's Motivational Value System® to further enhance your effectiveness in together serving Him? Explain your answers.

2. Journal Time: Make a list of special needs and/or times of year where your spiritual gifts employed together as a couple might be a special blessing to others. After you use your gifts together, come back and record what happened.

3. Prayer Time: Again, thank God for the way He has made ("wired") and gifted your spouse. Pronounce a blessing over them. And, ask God for opportunities to act on the list you put together in today's journal time.

Chapter Eight
Adoption vs Orphan Spirit

Forever His Child

Li Xiu Ying was a gift to her parents. But they didn't see it that way. They were living on the edge of poverty, as were many of their friends and neighbors in China's Qinghai Province. And like most other inhabitants of their remote village, they were hoping their first child would be a boy. They not only wanted a boy; their plan required a boy; one that would eventually take over their family "subsistence farm". Their meager plot of farmland was the means by which they could exist. It was also their retirement program. They knew some day they would no longer be able to do the back-breaking physical labor required to keep the farm productive. In addition to yielding their sustenance, their land barely yielded enough surplus which was sold or traded for other non-food needs and supplies.

To put it bluntly, a girl did not fit their simple strategy. It was quickly obvious to Li's parents she would not be living in their hut for long. She would be going somewhere to someone who could provide for her and address her physical issues.

Li's parents graciously chose to let her live, in spite of the superstitious urgings of some. "Life" was the only gift they could give her. They simply couldn't afford a girl, much less the surgery needed to repair her deformities. So, even though she had only been alive for a few weeks, the time had come for Li to be given away.

Spending what precious little money they had, her mother traveled a great distance merely to find an orphanage. The ones Li's mother knew of were Government sponsored but mostly unmonitored, and notoriously inadequate. Still, she hoped she'd find a good one that could provide the proper care for her baby girl including the operation(s?) she needed. And she hoped someday someone would adopt Li. It broke her heart to let her baby go, but she thought that was their only hope; for her and Li.

Having travelled far, Li's mother finally located an orphanage. From the outside, it looked acceptable. Kind people greeted her at the entrance. First impressions were good. As she relinquished her baby girl, Li's mother knew this was the last time she would ever see her.

The orphanage was barely adequate, yet "good" by the standards of its undeveloped province. But Li did not do well there. How could she? There was an overwhelming number of babies just like her; abandoned or given up. The care takers simply didn't have enough time for them all; time for them to receive the touch and affection each child desperately needed to thrive. And physically, Li was not doing well either. Her cleft lip and cleft palate made feeding times problematic and time consuming for those providing her care. There wasn't much they could do about her facial anomalies; the orphanage itself was living on the ragged edge of financial solvency. The best they could do was give her food and clothing; surgery was out of the question for now.

Somehow Li survived her early months, but as the years passed, she was quiet and withdrawn. Living in an orphanage was tough enough without the many dental issues and hearing complications caused by her cleft palate. As she grew, in spite of her body's setbacks it was obvious she was strong of spirit. She lived moment to moment in hopes of one day receiving not only her needed surgeries but a family as well. (Oh, how her heart ached to "belong".)

During her short life, Li watched many of her friends be adopted. Few of them ever returned; most she supposed, were staying with their new-found families in other wonderful countries. Through tears Li would often think, "No one will ever adopt me looking like this. I really am scary to most people. How will I ever get adopted if someone doesn't fix my mouth?" She experienced a level of rejection no five-year-old should ever have to deal with. And, her rejection wasn't merely a "sense"; it was real. She had been returned to the orphanage more than once. As it turned out, few people were equipped to handle the emotional issues that came with an abandoned, disfigured child. Nearly defeated, Li resigned herself to be an orphan.

Years came and went at the orphanage. As she grew older and more capable, Li decided to make the best of her existence in spite of her appearance. She expressed that desire by requesting permission to work with the orphanages' numerous babies. She knew the babies wouldn't even think about her disfigured mouth or the mangled words that proceeded from it. Her superiors approved her request then taught her how to change and launder re-usable cloth diapers. "It's a dirty job", Li thought. "But it is appropriate for someone like me." Li could neither be accused of giving up nor of thinking too much of herself.

Then one wonderful day one of the orphanage leaders, a kind woman named Wang Xiu Ying heard about a group of doctors coming to a village in another part of their province. As it turned out, the doctors were plastic surgeons specializing in cleft palate surgery. Li and Xiu (as this leader preferred to be called) both knew Li just <u>had</u> to get to the clinic where these visiting doctors would operate on as many patients as they could during their limited stay. Hopeful on Li's behalf, some of the leaders of the orphanage pooled their meager rainy-day funds to buy Li a round trip bus ticket to the clinic.

When the day for Li's trip finally arrived, many bows and heart felt tears were exchanged between Li, Xiu and other members of the orphanage staff. All were hoping that Li would be selected for the surgery. And they were hopeful it would not only correct Li's lip and palate but also start the process of healing the numerous emotional wounds she had suffered through the years. Even though her teenage years were now fast approaching, they still hoped she might find someone, better, some family that was willing to adopt and accept her. Perhaps the surgery would improve those odds.

At the bus stop, Li's designated bus was waiting for her. She was one of the last passengers to board. When she stepped on, everyone stared at her then quickly looked away. She immediately knew this was not going to be a comfortable ride. This bus was packed-full with people who would rather look away than show compassion. She wondered if the staff of the clinic would react to her the same way. The long ride to the clinic provided way too much time to ponder that thought.

Li's bus finally arrived at the stop closest to the clinic. While she gathered her belongings and waited her turn to disembark, Li attempted to conceal her appearance by keeping her head as low as possible. At this anxious moment in her life, she just didn't need the added rejection.

When she finally located the clinic, a surgeon just happened to be standing at its front door. He had just returned from the local farmer's market. At the threshold of the clinic Li met the first white person she had ever seen. A translator was called and with his help, Li learned the doctor preferred to be called, "Dr. Dave". In near shock, she thought to herself, "His skin isn't the color of mine! He's, uh, white!" Her reaction (rejection?) surprised even her. She hadn't even considered that the doctors might be of some skin color other than hers. In spite of her surprise and due to his lack of gasping at the sight of her cleft lip, Li was assured she was indeed in the right place.

Inside the clinic, after a quick initial examination of Li's mouth, Dr. Dave asked Li, "Where are your parents? We need to talk to them before we consider this surgery. We need their understanding and approval." With hung head and slumping shoulders Li haltingly and timidly replied, "I'm an orphan. I am alone." She was expecting shame and rejection from Dr. Dave. What she couldn't have foreseen was the rush of Spirit-empowered compassion flowing from Dr. Dave's heart; that compassion expressing itself through his watery eyes. Having sensed her pain, Dr. Dave quickly gathered himself, gave her a cautious side-arm hug and through the translator said, "You are exactly the kind of patient we are looking for! Let's get this done as soon as possible." Li was shocked. This was the first time a total stranger had not rejected her. Dr. Dave's acceptance was overwhelming. Li broke down and cried.

At his prompting, the translator inquired why she was crying, Li explained, "Never have I felt so much acceptance and love from someone I just met!" Dr. Dave mistakenly thought Li was weeping for joy because of the offered surgery. In his wildest imagination, he couldn't have dreamed her tears were due instead to his acceptance of her. When the translator explained Li's comments to him, Dr. Dave wept again.

The next day, Dr. Dave went to work on Li's mouth. He was an excellent surgeon. Over the decades of his practice, he had received many accolades from his peers and patients for his surgical skills and humanitarian work. Because of his vast experience, he was confident Li possessed great beauty; it was simply waiting to be revealed. It was no surprise to him when he was proved right. Having learned of her past history, he knew she already lived up to one meaning of her name: "brave". Now, surgery completed, she would live up to the other meaning of her name: "Elegant."

Li was told she could not go back to the orphanage until she fully recuperated. It took days for the pain to subside and about a week on top of that for the bandages to be reduced to a size she could manage on her own. Who could have known that Li's skill developed by changing numerous diapers would prepare her for changing her own surgical dressing....and maybe one day those of others.

Before Li left the clinic, Dr. Dave took one last look at her rapidly healing scars. His surgical skill was so acute, one could barely detect the pink traces of tissues still in the process of healing. Even Dr. Dave was struck by how well Li was recovering. He was also struck by how truly beautiful she now was. When she finally worked up the courage to look in the mirror, she saw her face was now complete…and for the first time, beautiful! Once more, it was Li's turn to weep.

Nearly five weeks had passed. Li had enjoyed the company of these grace-filled clinic people. It was hard for her to leave but she knew it was time for her to go back to the orphanage. She was filled with gratitude and appreciation but had little idea of how to express it. Instead of accepting an attempted bear-hug by one of the nurses, she merely smiled, bowed, then waved good bye.

At the bus stop, Li's designated, return-trip bus was waiting for her. She was one of the last passengers to board. When she stepped on everyone stared at her but then kept on staring. She was beautiful to look at. She immediately knew the ride going "home" would be more comfortable than the one that brought her to the clinic. This bus was packed-full with people who looked at her and accepted her appearance even though they had no idea of her heart or past.

When she returned to the orphanage the staff was shocked and pleased to see the beauty she had become. Xiu warmly greeted her and exclaimed, "Li, you really are elegant." Li was embarrassed by all the attention; it was unfamiliar territory for her. She loved the change Dr. Dave's skills had affected but it was going to take her a while to adjust to her new look. And in her heart, she hoped, "Even though I am older, now will someone adopt me?" It wasn't long until that question was answered.

A few weeks after her return, there was an uncommon commotion at the make-shift front desk. Some white people, "White like Dr. Dave," Li noted, had come to the orphanage looking for Li. The staff was excited as they learned that at Dr. Dave's prompting, these people wanted to adopt Li. Li cautiously contained her excitement as she wondered, "Really! My turn? Who are these people?" She would soon find out they were friends and financial supporters of Dr. Dave's. Being friends of Dr. Dave's meant they had to be good people. Being financial supporters of Dr. Dave's meant they were wealthy. "Jackpot!", on both accounts!

With the help of a translator for the next few days, her new mom and dad, Justin and Charissa Alderson interacted with Li. It didn't take long for their hearts to begin to connect. Justin and Charissa knew they had found the newest member of their family. When the paperwork was eventually completed, Li was officially released into Justin and Charissa's care. But there were still huge psychological adjustments to be made in Li's life.

In order to celebrate her adoption into their family, Justin and Charissa decided to fly their other three children to a five-star resort in Thailand. There they would meet their newest sister, Li.

When they all finally arrived at the resort, the Alderson family was celebrating but Li wasn't. She was struggling. For starters, she didn't understand their language. Further, she wasn't used to the abounding love the Aldersons affectionately gave each other through jovial hugs and back-slaps. Those expressions were unfamiliar and overwhelming to Li. It was all so hard for a lifelong orphan to process. Consequently, for the first few days at the resort, Li rejected every affectionate display of acceptance. It was difficult for any member of the Alderson family to express acceptance and love due in part to the language barrier and Li's inability to receive it.

In her soul, Li was suspicious this adoption might be short lived. She had had prior experience. Her suspicion couldn't help but have an adverse effect. The mere thought of all this love evaporating resulted in several outbreaks of moody anger. And this was just the start of Li's challenges surfaced by this opulent resort. Who could have foreseen the bewilderment and temptation the buffets would bring?

When it came to meal time which was "always" at this resort, it seemed to Li there were buffet tables everywhere. Never in her short life had she seen so much food! There were serving tables adorned with towering ice sculptures in whose shadows were myriads of salads nestled in small hills of sparkling ice, "To keep their varying ingredients crisp and fresh," she discerned. Li observed that some serving tables were dedicated to mind boggling arrays of cheeses and crackers; their arrangements being worthy of first prize, if there were such a competition. There were specialized stations dedicated to keeping soups steaming hot. If you wanted bread with your soup you wouldn't have to exert yourself at all as within a few short steps, linen draped tables were heaped high with fresh baked rolls and breads that had just arrived from the resort's massive ovens. The smell of those baked goods prompted many a guest to inhale deeply the almost-intoxicating aroma. Jams, jellies butter, cream cheese and various other spreads were offered in crystal bowls and heralded by a beautiful sign hinting, "Take all you want!"

This everyday-feast also included multiple tables of meat attended by servers standing at attention just outside the funnel-shaped amber glow of the inverted heat-lamps hung chest-high before them. Carving knife and oversized two-pronged fork in hand, the servers stood ready to custom-carve any beef, pork, lamb, turkey or chicken of one's choice. If the carvers sensed a guest was timid about portions, they would often encourage and delight the guest with a smile and a quip like, "You should have a bigger slice than that!" Li imagined, "This single buffet could alone feed the whole orphanage for weeks!"

And if all that wasn't enough, there were dessert stations offering every kind of ice cream, pudding, parfait, cake, cobbler or cookie you could imagine. "Just help yourself," an attendant said to Li, assuming she could understand every word of his version of English. There was more dessert than Li had ever seen.

The whole dining experience was overwhelming; Li just knew it was too good to be true. She suspected her new father's love and provision was conditional and therefore temporary. So, she resolved to at least be in control of the inevitable pain of rejection. To herself she reasoned, "If Justin is going to reject me, I will attempt to reject him first." Fearing that that inevitable rebuff was just around the corner, Li began preparing for her imagined return to the orphanage. She began stuffing dinner rolls into her pants, jacket pockets, shoulder-slung purse, and anything else she could use to transport them. Li thought, "If I am going to be sent back to the orphanage, it will not be without some of this delightful food. This 'too good to be true' feast can't possibly last. Any food that will not spoil quickly is fair game." When she was ready, she mimed to her family her intent to go back to her room; her concealed payload for this trip was maxed out. Back at her room, she hid her reserves in the closet. This behavior would be repeated over the next few days of her stay.

Li closed the door to her closet, then left her room. Confident in her food-storage plan she walked the many halls and staircases leading back to the dining area. When the meal time was "over", (was it ever really over?!) in response to a siblings' invitation, Li decided to check out one of the resort's many swimming pools.

The first one was indeed a wonderful pool, she enjoyed being there with her sister. But Li had learned there were multiple pools. With a sense of urgency motivated by the thought she might, any day now be sent back to the orphanage, Li decided to experience them all on her own. But it wasn't easy to find the second one; the resort campus was huge. After several unsuccessful attempts, Li finally did find a second pool. Nearly getting lost in the massive resort benefited Li with the realization she had the same freedom-to-explore offered all resort guests. When that reality dawned on her, she determined to find and play in every single one of their pools. And she decided to descend every single one of their water slides again and again and again. There was more exploration and fun in this one afternoon of her life than all the others put together. Li thought to herself, "This has been fantastic! But I am so hungry. Now I know why food is always available here!"

When this glorious "once in a life time", five-star-resort day concluded, Li should have slept like a proverbial baby. However, when they all turned in for the night, she couldn't sleep. Her bed was simply too clean and too comfortable for her to enjoy.

Day four dawned at the resort. Li was struggling with all the changes in her life. It helped immensely for her to meet a resort guest who just happened to be there for one day only and who just happened to speak Li's dialect. To Li, she seemed to come out of nowhere. And interestingly enough Li thought, she sure knew a lot about adoption. This mysterious guest also seemed to know "why?" the Aldersons could already love Li so much. Consequently, Li began to realize her new father and mother, this family and all it affords, was "hers and permanent." It was legal. It was done. She was adopted. She was accepted, forever! There would be no going back to the orphanage, period.

At a pause in their conversation, the mystery guest offered a treat. She said, "I am going to go get an ice cream cone, want one?" Li declined. As wonderful as ice cream sounded, it wasn't nearly as significant as the love her soul was now sampling. To herself she thought, "Could this all be genuine?" Mid thought, it dawned on Li she had not yet thanked her new-found friend for all the counsel she had provided. Li resolved to correct that oversight before she asked the whole new wave of questions now swirling in her soul. Li waited and waited, but the mystery guest never returned. Li wondered where she went or "why?" she would leave so abruptly. She wondered if she had somehow offended her friend but knew in her heart she hadn't. Now, Li was hoping she could either find another translator or learn English, fast. Either way she would have to ask her new family for answers to the rest of her questions. Eventually she would discover they were more than willing to provide answers. For now, she would have to accept their actions as testimony of their love and acceptance.

The more Li's mind pondered the counsel her mystery guest had provided, the more she realized and accepted the reality and permanency of her adoption. And the more her soul and demeanor changed. The Aldersons were also witnessing Li's change of heart, and it was good. Her new mom, dad, brothers and sister were all relieved and overjoyed that their prayers were obviously being answered. Li was accepting the profound truth that she was "home"; loved and fully accepted. That truth was changing her into the child of peace and joy she was eternally designed to be.

As the nature of this adoption increasingly took root, Li resolved to curtail thinking like an orphan. Due in part also to what she perceived was her siblings' experience, she was determined to fight off her thoughts of fear and doubt. She was sufficiently strong-minded, to pursue never again seriously doubting the love of her new-found father and mother. And, no longer would she be tempted by the thought to "merely exist". In fact, given the rapidly developing discovery of her true potential, she was now starting to think beyond her own needs to the needs of others. The genuine faith and prayers of the Alderson family were truly having an impact. Li was about to have two new families; the second would be eternal!

Still at the resort, fruit smoothie in hand, Li sat at the edge of one of the resort's luxurious pools. Hope was starting to well up within her as she dreamed about her future. While her feet bicycled the pool's surface Li thought to herself, "I am no longer an orphan! Maybe one day I'll become a doctor; maybe even a plastic surgeon. There are so many kids like me who desperately need healing, love, acceptance and 'yes' a family. God willing, I'll help and heal others." "God willing?", she thought. Where did <u>that</u> come from?"

As she reflected on possible answers to her self-posed question, deep within her heart, she knew she wanted the same grace-filled faith her new family shared. Though it seemed like everything was happening so fast, Li didn't feel hurried; she yielded. In her native tongue, with humble gratitude, she ventured her first prayer to her other new Father: "God, I know you are out there. Sending the Alderson family to me is partial proof. Through them, thank you for giving me another example of your love. If you are willing, please accept me then use me the rest of my life. I want to make a difference in the lives of other lost and broken ones." To herself she thought, "I hope that prayer worked." An instant answer was perceived through an overwhelming peace that pervaded her body, soul and spirit.

This very personal, pool-side revelation of the Heavenly Father's love and acceptance would lead Li down a life-path the likes of which she could have never imagined even a few short days ago. Secure in full-surrender, she did not stress over His timing in her life. Even now <u>she</u> sensed that her pilgrimage would soon reveal that God is Sovereign, His timing is perfect and that He had arranged her permanent place at the Alderson family table. And <u>He</u> knew His newly-adopted daughter, better this strong and elegant "princess" He had designed, would soon revel in the fact that her place at His table was, Forever!

Couples Daily Devotionals: Forever His Child

Day One:
1. Bible Reading: Galatians 3:26.
   Galatians 3:26 tells us we become children of God
   through faith in Jesus Christ. Have you become God's
   child through faith? Share with your spouse how that
   happened even if you have already done so and even if it
   was a long time ago. If you have children, grandchildren,
   nieces/nephews, tell them how you became a child of
   God through Christ: call them, write them, text, email
   them; whatever works.

2. Journal Time: Write out a commitment to share your
   conversion story to as many family members as possible.
   Who might be the first one you will share with?

3. Prayer Time: Pray together asking God to give you
   opportunities to share your conversion story with family
   members. Pray especially for those you would be most
   afraid to share with and/or those you think might not
   want to hear your story.

Day Two:
1. Bible Reading: In Galatians 3:13 we read that Christ paid
   the heavy price for us having the choice of being adopted
   into God's family.

   a. Are there any "hidden fees" we must pay for our
      adoption?

b. Is your answer to "1-a" more evident in what you profess or what you practice? Why?

2. Journal Time: Are there areas in your spiritual walk that reveal a belief in "hidden fees"? Record them as an exercise of renouncing them.

3. Prayer Time: Ask God's Spirit to identify any false beliefs about performance or practice based spiritual adoption i.e. legalism. Ask God to help you to ever increasingly understand how loved, accepted and forgiven you are in Christ.

Day Three:

1. Bible Reading: Romans 8:15 tells us we are not to live in fear. Why? Because we have been adopted into God's family through Christ's sacrifice by the Holy Spirit.

a. What connection do you see between being living as adopted children of God and dealing with our fears? (Hint: In II Timothy 1:7 we read that we have not received a spirit of fear but one of power, love and a self-control. Some versions read: "…and a sound mind.")

b. What are some of your most common/recurring fears? What might they reveal about your confidence in your salvation through Christ? What do your fears falsely imply about the nature/character of your heavenly Father?

2. <u>Journal Time</u>: Record your fears and what they reveal about your security in Christ; and what they negatively imply about your heavenly Father.

3. <u>Prayer Time</u>: Ask God to fill you with His Spirit in order to assist you in overcoming your fears. As for the Spirit of Truth to teach more about the nature and qualities of your Heavenly Father; He is perfect yet loves you dearly and deeply. Give Him praise for His love for you and your family.

Day Four:

1. <u>Bible Reading</u>: In Exodus 2:10 we read of Moses becoming the son of Pharaoh's daughter. Sometimes in some cultures people might be tempted to attach negative connotations to adoption. Do you have any negative feelings or thoughts about adoption? Do you have any negative thoughts about being adopted into God's family?

Moses was adopted. He is one of the most widely known and revered persons in world history/religion. God's might purpose was fulfilled through Moses. What might Moses' adoption reveal about God's view of adopted children? Also, do you think there any step-children or grandchildren in God's family? Explain.

2. <u>Journal Time</u>: Record your negative and positive feelings about adoption. If the Enemy has caused you to attach

negative ideas about being adopted into God's family, try to reduce those thoughts to words. Doing so just might help you gain greater peace, freedom, and a deeper awareness of how significant you are to God.

3. Prayer Time: Ask God to fulfill His purpose today and every day in you, your children and grandchildren. Ask the Spirit to help you identify any negative connotations you might have about being adopted. Express your praise for the secure place you hold in God's family.

Day Five:

1.   Bible Reading: In Ephesians 1:5 we read that God had predestined us to adoption. That is a profound theological concept to contemplate. What does it mean to you? In Ephesians 2:10 we read that we are God's workmanship created in Christ Jesus to do good works which God prepared for us to do before this world even began.

   a.   What does this reveal about how special you are to God? (Compare Ps. 139:16; Jer. 1:5)

   b.   What does this reveal about how special His purpose is in creating you? In preparing good things for you to do?

   c.   What evidence might you offer which shows you truly do believe you are forever His child?

2.   Journal Time: Record some "good works" (no matter how small/large) you think God would have you do. Make a plan

to start doing them right away while also trusting God's provision to do so.

4. <u>Prayer Time</u>: As a special, adopted child in the family of God, talk to God about fulfilling the purpose for which He created and adopted you. And, praise Him for His adoption of you.

Chapter Nine
Love Keeps No Record of Wrongs

It's a Record!

It seemed like such a small thing at first. But as the argument continued, the issues and emotions grew and expanded. Both were sure they had heard what the other swore they never said. Neither one really understood how they ended up with such animosity towards each other. But here they were again, Whitney in full attack mode, Jason in full retreat mode, inevitably to churn and fume. During the hours ahead, in the privacy of their own thoughts, each would revisit the argument countless times as they contemplated what they could have and should have said to the other.

This time it started on Sunday in the kitchen as brunch preparations were being made for their children and soon-to-arrive guests. Jason, Whitney and the kids had just returned from church. The kids were in their rooms putting away their Sunday school handouts and changing clothes. Jason and Whitney were in the kitchen with Whitney filling the role of chef and Jason as sous chef.

As he diced the onions for a huge omelet, Jason ventured, "Boy, the priest was all over the map this morning. I have no idea where he was going or what point he was trying to make. Did you get anything out of his message, honey?"

After taking some time to reflect on what she perceived to be another critical comment from Jason, Whitney couldn't help but come to the defense of her longtime family-friend. "Yes," she replied with a slight edge of irritation in her voice. "I did get something out of what he said. But I can see why you didn't. You were fidgeting and fussing by about the two-minute mark of his message. In that short period of time, you were already totally tuned out. And it's no wonder, I mean how can you honestly say you were listening when at the same time you were playing those frivolous games on your smart phone? Why can't you do one thing at a time? And why do you always have to be so critical of others?"

Jason was instantly in full opposition to the one he loved so dearly. To himself he deliberated, "Here we go again. How is it I so often end up on the opposite side of whatever the issue is? I wish we didn't fight like this."

His out loud response to Whitney went something like this: "Critical? You want critical!? Why are you always so critical of me? Every time I bring up something simply to share what is going on in my brain, you come to the defense of the other person or take the other side of whatever the issue might be. Why!? Can you tell me why!? It feels to me like you are more willing to defend others than me. How can I possibly go deeper with you in our marriage when time after time you attack me and defend whoever or whatever I am having issues with? Would you rather I share deeply with someone other than you?"

"Go deeper with someone else? Would you rather share deeply with someone else? Is there a 'someone else?' Is it that cute brunette at your office? Is that what you are really trying to tell me; you are having an affair?" Whitney had shifted from being slightly irritated to full-on attack mode. Her manner and allegations really caught Jason off guard.

"An affair?! Are you kidding me? I ask if you got anything out of this morning's message and you leap to the conclusion of adultery? How could you possibly accuse me of having an affair? How ridiculous!" As soon as his counterattack was out of his mouth, he knew he shouldn't have said it. How could she accuse him? Well, he had a previous history with pornography, so it wasn't too hard to take the leap from porn to an actual affair. But still, Jason was wondering, "How did we get to this issue?"

Whitney's response to Jason's verbal attack was nearly predictable. "I'm ridiculous? How could I accuse you of having an affair? Well... let me see now." Her sarcastic, demeaning tone only served to advance Jason's inner turmoil. Whitney continued, "You have admitted to multiple visits to porn sites. You have confessed them to me and promised to never do it again. But then time after time I have caught you on porn sites. Add to that the reality that some gorgeous brunette sits at a desk just outside your office door. Add to that her very stylish yet provocative attire. Add to that your interest in porn and 'voila!' Hmmm...how do you think I could accuse you of having an affair with someone else?"

Jason was now obviously hurt again. He was accepting the waves of cavernous condemnation coming from his deeply hurt and offended wife. Shame and disgrace swept over him in hot embarrassment. He withdrew. Gone was his assertiveness. Gone was his attack mode. He wondered, "How could I repeatedly visit porn sites? I really do love Whitney. There is no way I would ever betray her trust in real life. Why can't she see that? Will I ever be able to find the right words to express my devotion and commitment to her and have her believe me?"

Whitney sensed Jason was withdrawing. But her anger was just starting to spool up. "Don't you dare pull back from me, mister! We are finally talking about the real issue here: your adultery! That's what it is, adultery. Oh, maybe not adultery with the brunette bimbo outside your office door, but you have imagined fornication with every two-dimensional woman you could find on the internet. You disgust me! You embarrass me! If people only knew the real 'man' you are, they too would be disgusted."

Guilt, hurt, pain, self-condemnation, and anger were now welling up to historic levels in his soul but he knew, at this moment, he couldn't say anything. From past experience, he knew that whatever words he offered in defense, those same words would be volleyed back in his face. He just had to stand there and take it. But if ever there was a time he wanted to escape conflict, it was especially, definitely, now.

Meanwhile, Whitney continued her verbal tirade. And Jason was in full surrender mode, instinctively perceiving that any logical response would only cause more trouble. He also knew that if he re-engaged in the argument it would most likely be to "win" the argument and that nothing good could possibly come from such a counterattack. So, he withdrew completely but not before he meekly responded to her insults. Jason said, "I am sorry I even mentioned anything about this morning's message. I'm going to go use the computer." And with that he walked out of the kitchen.

"Don't you dare leave me here to prepare this whole meal by myself! You are the one who invited the Jacobs and the Smiths to brunch. You get right back in this kitchen and help me. I am not doing this by myself!" The degree of Whitney's anger reflected much more hurt and pain than could be caused by a need to defend the priest's message. But even she wasn't sure why she chose now, when company was on the way, to get so upset over old issues.

In response to her demands, Jason merely said, "Whatever." He didn't go back in the kitchen to help and he didn't go into the computer room. He really had to steel himself in order to not answer the pseudo-comforting siren call of porn sites. Rather than re-trace his steps back into the battle field of the kitchen, he passively yet aggressively informed Whitney he would set the table. Whitney decided to back off and maybe regroup for later reengagement.

The air in their house was filled with tension, but Jason and Whitney managed to prepare the meal without letting their kids know, they hoped, just how angry they both were and how badly they were both hurting.

By the time company arrived, the unhappy couple had calmed down to the point of being civil to each other. Their guests could have never surmised how bad things had been prior to their arrival. However, the guests did notice that: The table setting was nice. The food was nice. The conversation was nice. The kids were nice. Jason and Whitney were nice. Typical of two well-trained religious people, everything on the surface appeared to be "nice" even though everything under the surface wasn't. When the food was gone, and conversations with their guests fully played out, the Sunday afternoon chores and schedules began demanding attention; Monday morning was merely hours away. It was time to begin the elongated process of saying "good bye."

With pleasantries including numerous thank-yous sufficiently exchanged, their company finally gathered up their belongings and their kids, then left. Relief! Jason and Whitney had succeeded at hiding their fight and their pain. No one, they thought, picked up the unresolved tension between them. They had fooled them all.

After the front door of their lovely (nice?) home was finally closed, they looked at each other with gratitude; both were thankful they could conceal their marital animosity and thereby preserve their happy image. But neither one wanted to speak first. As they were clearing the table, Whitney eventually took the initiative.

"I don't like fighting like this," she said in her best politically correct tone. "It seems we just start getting into whatever the real issue is but then you retreat leaving me with no idea what to do with my anger. It seems to me whenever I bring up the past, our arguments never bring any resolution or progress." She was trying real hard, but unsuccessfully so, to be conciliatory

Jason was starting to sense her anger was already on the rise again. Because it was. Whitney noticed her "edge" as well and chose to tone it down. Jason was grateful she didn't break the meager peace they were experiencing, but he couldn't help getting in one last jab of justice.

"We don't make progress because every time we fight, you go backwards. How can we go forward if you always go backward? That makes no sense!"

She responded defensively, "What do you mean we go backwards? I strongly disagree!"

"Well, every time we fight, you have to bring up one or more of my past failures, right? You just did it a couple of hours ago. In a typical fight, I confess my sin, while you never confess anything. Usually, I ask for your forgiveness, you grant it but then don't <u>leave</u> it cancelled. Inevitably I know you will bring up again some supposedly forgiven failure of mine. In fact, every time we fight you get historical!"

Whitney was quick to correct him, "You mean 'hysterical' not 'historical'. And I do not get hysterical, I was merely engaging!"

Jason corrected her correction. "No, I meant what I said; 'historical'. You always bring up my past failures when we fight. It's like you are a walking 'pdf' of my faults." In his current conflict mode, Jason could have recited an itemized list of <u>her</u> record of his wrongs. Neither realized the different ways they kept that detailed record on each other; a record of every hurt, pain, and failure-to-follow-through.

Fearful the kids would overhear their fighting, Whitney tried to de-escalate this fight. She did so by changing her behavior in hopes that Jason would now interpret her as a bit more self-controlled. She offered the following words: "I am sorry for doing whatever hurts you, Jason. I don't know why I do what I do when we fight, do you? And maybe even more importantly, no one has ever taught me practical steps on how to fight <u>and</u> permanently forgive. Jason, do you know how to truly forgive?" Their mutually exchanged quizzical looks communicated neither knew.

Truth be told, neither Jason nor Whitney knew why, when in conflict, they behaved the way they did. Sometimes their behaviors surprised even them. And they both believed they did not get married to really hate each other but rather to really love each other. But the absence of healthy conflict resolution skills modeled by their parents, coupled with the lack of any actual "how to fight fair" training, left them both adrift in an "ocean of emotions" and uncertainty whenever conflict was enjoined. So, they both wondered, "Why do we keep a record of wrongs? What good does it do? How can we make peace and truly forgive? Is there a difference between trust and forgiveness?" They agreed that those were four great questions that had to be answered. They were certain there were many more peacemaking questions that required answers. So, they both agreed to begin a "getting answers" journey which started by talking to their priest. If their priest couldn't offer practical steps or couldn't give them direction where to get those practical steps, Jason promised Whitney that he would keep searching until he <u>did</u> find answers. If nothing else, he was determined to set a record for gaining new insight on how to fight fair. And, as a good father, even though neither he nor Whitney had had a good example in their families of origin, Jason knew their children deserved a healthier example of resolving conflict without getting "historical". After all, they reasoned, two people who had personally experienced true forgiveness, who were so much in love, should know how to fight and truly forgive. As ones whose record of wrongs had been cancelled by the Savior, they of all people should be able to model this for their kids, their friends and anyone else for that matter. Right?

Couples Daily Devotionals: It's a Record!

Day One:

1. <u>Bible Reading</u>:   Read I Corinthians 13:5.

   a.   What actions depicted in this verse typify true love? What are the opposites of these actions?

   b.   In your marriage, are you practicing any "opposites of love"?

   c.   What loving actions could you either/both of you improve on?

2. <u>Journal Time</u>: List the loving actions you need to improve on and the opposites you need to dump.

3. <u>Prayer Time</u>: Ask God to help you be more loving, like Him. Ask Him to help you practice the action of love not the opposites of love.

Day Two:

1. <u>Bible Reading</u>: Read Matthew 5:9

   a.   How are peace-makers described in this verse? How might being "family" and peace-making connected?

    b. What connection might there be between peace-making and God's blessing in one's marriage?

2. <u>Journal time</u>: Are there issues in your marriage that have not been resolved? Will you list them and make a commitment to resolve them?

3. <u>Prayer time</u>: Ask God to help you act like His children especially when it comes to making peace with each other.

Day Three:

1. <u>Bible Reading</u>: Read Hebrews 12:15.

    a. Do know of any bitter married couples? How do you know they are bitter? How do you think they got that way?

    b. What effect has their bitterness had on their children? On you?

2. <u>Journal Time</u>: What might be some good strategies for not becoming bitter towards each other? Record your answers along with a commitment to not become bitter.

3. <u>Prayer Time</u>: Ask the Holy Spirit to fill you and remove any bitterness you have in your heart towards God or each other...or anyone else. Thank God that He is not bitter towards you.

Day Four:

1. <u>Bible Reading</u>: Read Luke 23:34.

   a. What is the difference between "positional" forgiveness (e.g. Father forgive <u>them</u>) and "transactional" forgiveness (e.g. "I forgive you" OR "please forgive me")?

   b. In view of Christ's example in Luke 23:34, should you ever withhold forgiveness of those who have offended you including your spouse? How might withholding forgiveness lead to keeping a record of wrongs?

2. <u>Journal Time</u>: Record any forgiveness you need to extend to your spouse (and/or other family members). Beginning with this list, make a commitment to stop keeping a "list" on others. You might even want to write this list on a separate piece of paper so you can dispose of it when you are done writing it.

3. <u>Prayer Time</u>: If forgiving those who have deeply hurt and/or disappointed you is especially hard to do, ask God for the strength to forgive. Thank God for forgiving you every time you ask.

Day Five:

1. <u>Bible Reading</u>: Read Luke 15:11-24.

   a. Did the wayward son's father bring up the son's record of wrongs against him?

   b. Why do you think the father didn't bring up the son's record of wrongs?

   c. In view of the father's treatment of his son, if your spouse expresses sorrow for past sins, is it ever appropriate to "punish" your spouse by withholding forgiveness? What might motivate one to withhold forgiveness?

2. <u>Journal Time</u>: If you haven't done so in a previous daily devotional, write down the names of those people you and/or your spouse need to be reconciled to. If you have done so, review your reconciliation progress praising God for forward progress and/or noting needed "action steps".

3. <u>Prayer Time</u>: Pray over/for opportunities to be reconciled to those who have offended you or you have offended. Even if those so listed aren't ready to be reconciled, ask God to help you maintain a heart of reconciliation (positional forgiveness) while waiting for the Holy Spirit to work in the hearts of those who don't want to be reconciled to you. Ask God to heal those relationships (transactional forgiveness).

Chapter Ten
Owning Who God Made You to Be

Who Will Help Us?

Bruce was raised in a Christian home. Dorsey was too. As children raised in America, they both had received love from their parents. They weren't sure they could describe what that love looked like and felt like; they just knew they had received it. Now please be aware, dear reader, this love they sensed expressed itself in considerably different home cultures.

Bruce's parents were raised by what some might call, "depression era Oakies." From generation to generation their parenting style revolved mainly around teaching children, "right from wrong" as well as "day to day survival" in a broken economy. They did indeed survive but with the scarcest of fare and minimal material possessions. For instance, Bruce could recall their typical Christmas celebration which consisted of each child receiving an orange, a few whole walnuts and one piece of hard candy. That was the entirety of the Christmas presents Bruce's parents could afford their seven children.

There were no marriage seminars or parenting classes, at least none that they were aware of, during this stage in what was then both "post and pre" world war America. As a result, Bruce's parents rarely did more than teach him Biblical values including honesty and hard work. The challenge of providing for a large family meant there wasn't time to do much more than give an honest day's work. Bruce's parental role models managed to make their primary lessons "stick". However, an unintended consequence of their unavailability was this: Bruce grew up with a set of gnawing, unanswered, very personal, identity questions.

Even thru his midlife, these identity questions covertly crawl-ed around in his consciousness on the back of what he came to think of as a lizard in a huge, virtual wood pile. (That is indeed an odd thought; it is strange what the mind will sometimes do. But it made sense given a childhood memory of his. Bruce could still vividly recall a huge pile of oak logs behind the house he grew up in. The logs were cut and hand-split with an ax, to perfect sizes for their wood burning stove. He could remember catching and playing with the lizards that used the wood pile as their private apartment complex. Often times a wood-pile tenant would emerge, then resting on all fours, it would just start doing "pushups". Why? As a child, he had no idea. He simply thought it was funny that lizards would do pushups. Were reptiles really in to physical fitness? Or could it be they were trying to impress somebody? If so, who?)

Anyway….

At the most unexpected times Bruce's imagined "question-lizard" would crawl out from the darkest, most labyrinthine corners of his mind. Exposed, it would pose, then just seem to perch there frozen in plain view of his mind's eye. This sun-baked question-lizard's casual four-legged posture and stare implied a purpose; mock him. When the lizard's inevitable accompanying cache of questions would emerge, it seemed to Bruce they didn't come from his mouth, as one might suspect. Rather, like comic strip thought-bubbles they would just pop-up atop his head, then like lost helium balloons, drift away unanswered. And those thought-bubble questions would be launched with perfect metronome-like timing at the highest point of every reptilian pushup. The result was maximum effect.

The personalized questions sounded like: (First push up) "Who am I, anyway? (Second pushup) Am I smart? (Third push up) Am I creative? (Fourth push up) Am I caring? (Fifth push up) I have been 'me' all my life. I only see life through my eyes. What's it like to be on the other side of 'me'?". On and on the penetrating, projectile like, thought-bubble questions would drift away, from this seemingly tireless reptile.

In his mind, Bruce could almost see the eyes of the question-lizard interrogating him as each question was launched precisely at the zenith of each push up. Sadly, this seeming recurring reptilian regimen rarely rendered answers; only questions. At the end of this routine, the question- lizard (Was it a small skink like the ones from the family wood pile?) would re-gather all the supposedly lost, previously launched, customized thought-bubble questions. He would collect them then retreat to Bruce's mental wood pile only to re-emerge, at some, painful, unexpected or inopportune time to once again harangue Bruce.

Now, Bruce had taken various assessments throughout his life most of which pegged him as an overachieving, driven, ambitious "go getter". He felt those results were indeed accurate; well mostly. But what about his desire to counsel and coach people? How did that fit? He thoroughly enjoyed helping others improve their lives, marriages, and families. Unparalleled fulfillment came for Bruce when life-coaching others, even if they didn't ask for it. Doing so was an expression of his care and compassion.

Then there was his deep interest in the sciences like: biology, chemistry, physics, and math. And he occasionally enjoyed researching some new corporate technology. How did those disciplines fit in with the typical results from the multitude of assessments he took?

Typically, his emotional/relational-batteries were recharged by being alone. Being with people for longer periods of time usually drained him. What might this reality mean?

So, as he had done much of his life, he continued to wonder, "How in the world do my interests in people and my interests in the pure sciences fit into the typical 'over-achiever' portrait of me?" Also, for most of his life Bruce thought himself to be:

- Athletic but not creative.
- Musical, but not musically gifted.
- Funny but a few people had told him too often he was merely annoying.

With these and other competing and counterproductive thoughts, it was no wonder he often thought to himself, "Who am I, really?"

Now, Dorsey, having been raised in a more secure home environment had significantly more self-awareness. She knew who she was in part due to her parents' nurturing which included many opportunities to risk; to try and succeed. When she didn't succeed she was taught, "You merely received 'feedback'. Now improve on what went right and leave what didn't." Her parental mentors told her, "Failure is not to be personalized; neither is it to be considered pervasive nor permanent." (When you are raised in a home with this kind of "grace"; with sufficient acceptance, sensed security, and attributed/deserved significance, it is much more likely you will feel loved and find it easier to give love, like Dorsey.)

It riled Dorsey to no end when members of Bruce's family of origin would publicly disrespect him. It literally grieved her to see his parents and siblings occasionally treat her beloved husband so poorly. To her, being just, right and fair were paramount in any relationship, period. Anything other than this was, well, tantamount to hatred. Besides, she reasoned, what possible good thing can come from being so condescending to another human being? A far better pursuit is to build others up according to their needs.

It was only natural then that Dorsey often loved Bruce via verbally building him up. She wanted him to know often, how much she loved him and that her love for him was dear and deep. She expressed her love by accepting him as he was. And yet she loved him so much she couldn't leave him languishing in his uncertain identity. She wanted him to be as confident as she knew he was competent. Additionally, by building him up with sincere observations of his character, nature and yes abilities, she hoped he would be more at peace with himself. After all, isn't peace of mind and soul what the Master Craftsman desires for His creations? Her encouragement was a constant in his life. Often times she would remark, "Bruce, in so many ways you aren't like other men." She intended her encouragement to help him own the man she knew him to be. But that was an uphill battle.

- She could see his ability to fill just about any role that was needed at home, work or church; he didn't see anything special about that. After all, when you expect yourself to do it all, you aren't pleased, impressed or surprised when you do. That's just what's expected.

- She could see his creativity; he knew he couldn't draw or paint.

- She loved to hear him play the guitar and sing. He could hear his former band leader criticize him for not playing every chord crystal clear every time. And soloes, were often entrusted to various band members, but not him unless it was a small, inconsequential part of the song.

- She loved his playfulness and quick wit. He could still hear his siblings and elementary school teachers mock these abilities telling him to "sit down and be quiet."

- She loved to hear him speak at his corporate gatherings because he was so, well, "good!" He would recall his misspoken words and all the people who didn't appreciate what he said; translate: both post-speech critics.

Now mind you, it was rather remarkable that Bruce was so well adjusted and such a great leader of his company. "By the grace of God," he often remarked to those who praised his performance.

Well years passed and the company experienced much success with Bruce at the helm. But they weren't settled with solely celebrating passed achievements. Various psychological, personality and performance assessments were routinely required of Bruce and his team in order to improve their effectiveness, communication and conflict management skills. A culture of supportive criticism and self-improvement reigned. Therefore, assessments were viewed as a welcome and healthy part of his company's leadership development.

Bruce felt that most of these assessments mainly measured one's behavior. Over time a continuously evolving thought was forming in his mind. It sounded something like this: "I wonder what is driving the behaviors being measured by these assessments?"

It wasn't until Bruce's company had its leadership team take the Strength Deployment Inventory* that his continuously evolving thought was addressed. And to his amazement, at nearly the same instant, his mental "question lizard" was finally captured and quieted, but not entirely eliminated. Through the training and assessment results, Bruce had discovered and more importantly started to own the reality that he was indeed able to fill just about any role his company required. "How about that!", he pleasantly admitted to himself. He still knew he wasn't perfect but now he had better understanding of himself and others.

The Soul Diagnostic Inventory (the SDI® assessment actually reveals issues in the soul) had also revealed his weaknesses. (Bruce had already intuitively hired people to fill in the gaps exposed by his weaknesses.) Having taken two additional assessments (Strengths Portrait® and Overdone Strengths Portrait®) that measured his strengths as well as what it looked like when he overused his strengths, this assessment-triad seemed to reveal Bruce still wasn't fully owning how his Creator designed him. He began to ponder, "Dorsey was right, once again. Why don't I listen to her more? (That was a great question that deserved greater exploration!) What is still keeping me from owning who I am? How does my family of origin affect me owning or not owning who I am? What lies have I believed about myself? Where did these lies originate from? Life has brought pain and serious wounds, how do these realities figure into my identity and the 'inside of the cup' as some ancient historical documents have described the 'soul'?"

Well, admittedly, the imaginary "question lizard" was doing pushups again, but this time it was not a hopeless mental workout. Instead, Bruce was filled with a joyous desire to further pursue this rewarding self-discovery. His first steps on this trek had yielded greater insight than he had expected. His appreciation for how uniquely and wonderfully the Master Designer had created and crafted him was now in full-bloom.

Post workshop, parked at his desk, pouring again over the assessment results, to himself he thought, "Wish I would have known this years ago. It would have helped me so much, not to mention those around me. I wonder what the next steps are for embracing then capitalizing on who the Master Craftsman created me to be? (What a wise question!)

Who will help me?" And then with even greater love and appreciation for his amazing Dorsey he thought, "Who will help us?"

Couples Daily Devotionals: Owning Who God Made You To Be

Day One:

1. <u>Bible Reading</u>: Jeremiah 1: 4-7.

    a. How long did God know of His "blueprint" for creating Jeremiah? What does that tell you about God's design of and purpose for Jeremiah? What are some implications of these same realities for you and your spouse, i.e. what does it say about God's design and purpose for you; your spouse?

    b. How did Jeremiah respond when God shared His foreknowledge with Jeremiah…about Jeremiah's design and "destiny"? Personalize Jeremiah's response i.e., how will you respond to God's design of you?

2. <u>Journal Time</u>: List a minimum of five things you like most about your spouse.

3. <u>Prayer Time</u>: Ask God to help you both have greater value and humble acceptance of the way God created each of you. Take time to thank God for His design and destiny for your spouse. Pray also for your loved ones that they too would accept and enjoy how God made each one of them.

Day Two:

1. <u>Bible Reading</u>: Ephesians 2: 1-10.

    a. Pay special attention to verse 10. In the original language, Greek, the word translated "workmanship" is poe-ay-mah. It is the word we get our word, "poem" from. What does this tell you about God creating you? (Hint: In literature, what are some crucial ingredients for a great poem? Or in art, what are some crucial elements of a masterpiece?)

    b. After having read these verses together, if you haven't entrusted your life to the Master Designer, will you do so now? (See appendix A.) If you haven't or don't want to take this wonderful step, why not?

2. <u>Journal Time</u>: Note any particular response/reaction you each have to acknowledging you are a master piece of God. Note also any response/reactions to "honoring" and blessing your spouse.

3. <u>Prayer Time</u>: Thank God specifically for making you one of his "masterpieces". Thank Him for the masterful way He made your spouse. Honor your spouse by invoking God's blessing on those things you specifically mention. (Examples: "God I thank you that you made my spouse so concerned about what is fair, right, just." "Thank you for their attention to detail." "Thank you, God, for their concern for others." "Thank you, God, for their ability to get things done." …. today please help them see an opportunity to use those abilities to help others and bring You glory today." Cf Ephesians 5:16)

Day Three:

1. <u>Bible Reading</u>: Philippians 4:8-9

   a. Would you consider this list to be reflective of how you typically "think" about your spouse? Why or why not? What "benefits" are there to adhering to this commanded thought life; to not doing so? Can you give any examples from daily life or media life (TV shows, movies) that model this "thought life" command? Remember, we are God's workmanship.

   b. So, when you think negatively/critically about your spouses' qualities, and the results of your own Strength Deployment Inventory*, what opinion(s) might it convey about God's creation?

2. <u>Journal Time</u>: Record a commitment to adhere to the "thought command" of Philippians 4:8-9. Check up on your success, by reading this commitment out loud together on this same day next week.

3. <u>Prayer Time</u>: Share with each other some of the more negative stereotypes you may have mentally recorded about each other. What "benefits" are there to keeping such a record? Ask each other for any needed forgiveness.

Day Four:

1. <u>Bible Reading</u>: I Corinthians 12: 7-11

On top of being a masterpiece of God, you are also specifically "gifted" by God via the Holy Spirit. Specifically note verse 11. What are some of the implications for you? Your spouse? What might be some of the benefits of God "determining" how He would design you? (e.g. What Motivational Value System® and spiritual gift(s) did He give you?)

2. <u>Journal Time</u>: Make note of the results of your Strength Deployment Inventory* and/or the spiritual gifts you each have. On this same day next week, come back to this page to note [with as little or much detail you like] the way God has "hard wired" you and/or spiritual gifts were used of God.

3. <u>Prayer Time</u>: Before God, in prayer, acknowledge each other's spiritual gift(s), as well as natural talents/abilities…taking note of how those giftings/talents/abilities have specifically blessed you and others. Also ask God for opportunities to use those giftings/talents/abilities today.

Day Five:

1. <u>Bible Reading</u>: Psalms 139: 14-16.

Read this passage in the Message translation. (You can look it up online at one of many sites, like Biblegateway.) Based on these and other Scriptures on this week's topic, who knows you best/most? And He still loves you more than words can express! (cf I John 3:1) What are some practical ways, towards your spouse, you can model God's love and acceptance?

2. Journal Time: Ask your spouse for some ideas you can apply to daily demonstrate your love and acceptance of him/her. Refer to this page often!

3. Prayer Time: Thank God for His very deep, intimate knowledge of you coupled with the reality that He still loves you "lavishly" (I John 3:1). Ask Him to help you see His daily demonstrations of this great love for you. Also, ask Him to give you the creativity to daily demonstrate your love and acceptance of your spouse.

Chapter Eleven

Faith Filled Risks and You

Hope's first husband had passed away long before either had planned. The void left in her heart was hard for her to face, much less express. The atypical incident resulting in his premature death made it even harder to process. Here's how it happened.

The twice daily route his logging truck would take usually started at a remote mountain-top loading zone. There his trailer would be loaded to the max. He never lost his admiration for the log handlers' ability to position each log. "Almost like match sticks," he would think to himself as he watched their amazing precision. He was thankful they took their job seriously. His destination? The corporate warehouse on the valley floor. There, his pine-log payload would be transferred into a shipping container which would in turn be loaded on a rail car en-route to Asia.

In anticipation of the serpentine, brake-challenging road ahead, Hope's first husband was executing his predictable, memorized, pre-run safety routines. The company-approved gross maximum load configuration was precisely adhered to, but he was known to always give it one final inspection. He was cautious, methodical and pre-dictable. "Leave nothing to chance," was his motto. He was trained by the best and believed what he was taught: "There is only one way to do things right, the company way."

On that fateful day, one that changed his and Hope's life forever, his routine inspection did not reveal a hair-line crack in the front left upright of his trailer. As the final log of this load was placed, no one could have foreseen the chaos about to be unleashed. As he made his way down the far side of the trailer, headed for the truck's cab, the hair line fracture cracked and grew to the point of total structural failure. Instantly several of the logs rolled off the top of the load and on top of him. It crushed him. There is no way he could have moved fast enough to avoid it. To this day no one including the corporate investigators can explain why it happened. And it all happened so fast! There was no time for anybody to do anything to save him. One moment he was standing there, the next moment he was just "down", as a coworker explained. When the incident was being reported to the company's safety investigators, each loading-zone employee expressed that they felt shock and unjustifiable shame when the accident occurred; they had all just stood there. The investigators concluded that their inaction was due in part to the understandable shock and denial associated with the traumatic event.

When the tragic news reached Hope, she was devastated. She understandably progressed through each of the five steps of grieving, even though she couldn't always tell you what they were. For months, as she grieved, "the steps" as they came to be known, took her on a daily emotional roller coaster ride. She never knew moment by moment, much less day to day, what part of the ride she was going to experience. But even as she experienced those serious ups and downs, her friends, college age children and extended family were continuously comforted by the overflow of her courage. They saw her faith that God would, someday, as He always did, work all

things together for the good of those who love Him. No one could
doubt she loved Him with all her heart. Her mature faith was tested,
and her trust proved to be more than mere belief; others had seen it
in action. She obediently grieved but she grieved as one with solid
hope. One couldn't help but be touched by the uncommon peace
and resolve she possessed, even in the midst of this untimely
tempest.

She was not super human, though. The passing did wound her,
deeply. The loss evoked soulish questions like, "How am I going to
move forward without my calm and cautious husband? Next time I
stand at one of life's crossroads, (like this one!) who is going to
stand in the gap for me? Who will tell whoever I am might be
dealing with, 'We need more time before making such a difficult
decision as....'?"

Her mind (or was it her heart?) could pose a bushel basket of
bothersome questions. Sometimes just thinking about her circumstances would cause pain that no general practitioner could even
begin to diagnose. After all, her pain wasn't the symptom of some
disease or dysfunction; it was due to her husband's death. The
wound was deep, the pain excruciating. Yet in her heart, at levels
deeper than any outer wound, she still submitted to the Sovereign
One she so revered. Sometimes she called Him "Papa." And whatever today's challenge was, she knew they could and would really
talk it out! She usually carried, but not exclusively so, the "out
loud" portions of their dialogue. Sometimes they would talk in the
lonely hours of the night. Often times they would talk during the
day even as she drove around town to her various appointments.
The people of her small mountain town were used to seeing her lips
move at unusually long traffic stops. They knew she was most likely
talking to Papa, (as she intimately called Him) redeeming what
might otherwise be wasted time. They knew that she knew how
precious every moment of every day was and is.

Well, time passed. Her soul's wound mended, mostly. The
internal scar was huge but honorably healthy. She knew she wanted
to be married again, but it was just so hard to even think of taking
those risks.

Then one day when she attended a well-advertised gathering at a
local bass club, it happened. The advertised topic that had sufficiently enticed her to attend was "When and how to use rip baits."
The well-written flyer triggered fond childhood recollections of

hearing her Dad enthusiastically talk about his latest fishing trip. During his reports, she would sometimes ask if she could join him on his next trip. He would usually tell her, "Next time", but "next time" never seemed to arrive. By the time she was old enough to be safe on such a trip, she was no longer interested in actually going fishing but she loved to be with her father and hear his stories when he returned. So much of bass fishing was a mystery to her and as an adult, she had vowed that someday she would learn. As it turned out, a long time would pass before that promise was even recalled.

"Yeah, go figure…Hope at a bass club meeting." She imagined her friends making such a curious comment, when they found out she planned to attend. But her adventuresome spirit urged her on to take the risk. She loved to learn. In fact, she loved to entertain new ideas and concepts no matter what the topic. "Eclectic" best defined her insatiable hunger for information with "experiential knowledge" holding premium value in her soul.

The pursuit of bass fishing would prove to be one of many new things she was now free to experience; one of many things her deceased husband had avoided. To him bass fishing was a waste of time and money. Consequently, it had been filed in the "not logical or practical" waste bin. In contrast, bass fishing was something she had always wanted to explore; it was on her bucket-list. When she heard that a well-respected local guide was going to lecture on rip bait techniques, she was definitely interested. A trailing thought was something along the lines of, "What in the world is a rip bait anyway? I remember Dad talking about them. Well, with so many great lakes around our town, I guess it's about time I found out. What have I got to lose? Go give rip baits a try! You might even own one someday if it doesn't require a permit." She could definitely be described as "curious".

And lately, her curiosity seemed to know no bounds, possibly due in part to the passing of her devoted yet usually-not-curious husband. However, it was also probable that some credit for this new unchained enthusiasm for knowledge was due in part to her late husband. To be more specific, early in their marriage he did some well-researched financial planning that included a life insurance policy. When he acquired the policy, he had lectured her: "I know the premiums are especially large at this season in our life. I know you think it is too much. I know (boy he knew a lot) if something happened to me, you feel you would be safe in the care of others.

But I am not comfortable with such uncertainty. Furthermore, you and I both know you can't trust the emotional, flowery promises of others should my departure prove to be untimely. If I am gone ahead of my schedule, I want to know you are well cared for." When that last thought was offered, she thought to herself, "When you are gone your 'schedule' will go with you, and I'll still be fine." When his lecture concluded, in her own mind she had said, "OK, so he isn't as romantic and trusting as I am, but he is way more pragmatic." As foreseen, his planning resulted in a significant payout; she was void of any financial cares and truly grateful for her husband's pragmatism.

Well, the day of Hope's much anticipated bass lecture finally arrived. The meeting began on time with the club president offering a respectful but short introduction. Who wants to waste time when such an expert is here, now, and ready to spill his fishing secrets? As the expert's lecture began, Hope thought his message intriguing, even though he didn't have the oratory skills of her pastor. But his lack was more than made up for by his enthusiasm. As his instruction progressed, she began to realize she had had no idea there could be so much difference between just going fishing and actually catching bass. "Really?" she thought, "you have to have the right pole, reel, line, leader and knot? I don't plan on being a tournament pro!" She had recently learned they actually have tournaments! And you can win money.... big money! On the national scale, consistent winners earn millions! "Wow!" she privately exclaimed, "I had no idea bass fishing was such big business!"

Without much forewarning, the guide ended his lecture but promised to return someday to enlighten them all about jerk-baits and crank-baits. The club meeting was officially over. Cookies and coffee had been offered to those who wanted to linger for an impromptu Q and A with the self-proclaimed "king of rip baits."

Almost everyone else was now standing; she was still seated but about to stand. Her delay was prompted by contemplating an amusing thought about whether "jerk" baits and "crank" baits were intended to describe the lure or the angler using them. "Anyway, time to get up," she thought. She leaned forward to retrieve her purse from beneath the seat immediately in front of her, but before she could shift her weight to stand, a nice man sat down next to her. He welcomed her, introduced himself, then asked her, "Is this your first time here?" She noted that he was neither threatening, nor was there anything necessarily remarkable or distasteful about his approach or appearance. His was your typical "face in the crowd." Not even remotely interested in another relationship yet, she was a bit taken back by his unexpected arrival and somewhat blunt introduction. Silently she wondered, "Is this guy just being friendly or is he hitting on me?" He benignly offered to get her coffee and cookies; she made up some reasonable sounding excuse about not drinking caffeine this late at night. He offered to buy her pie and decaffeinated coffee at a local restaurant; but she shared her just-invented policy of not going out with any man she just met. That excuse sounded plausible, but just a bit more contrived. He asked if she would return for the jerk and crank bait lecture. She answered with a vague response prompted by her rising level of nervousness and suspicion that he was in fact coming on to her. She tried to recall long forgotten and probably old-fashioned dating protocols; she wasn't sure how to respond to him. In fact, with her heart now racing she was thinking, "What was his last question?" Uncharacteristically flustered, she was failing to calm her heart to a normal rhythm. Her wild imagination pictured her laying on the floor where someone who had attached a defibrillator to her was yelling, "Clear!" (It was apparently, the rescuer's third and final attempt to stabilize her now fluttering heart.)

Back in real time, she hastily gathered herself, muttered a semi-gracious goodbye to Mr. Average then bolted for door. Once outside, like an Olympic speed walker, she was covering the path to her car in record time. As she swiftly made her way towards her car, she had to cover her mouth in an unsuccessful attempt to restrain the waves of near convulsive giggles emerging from the depths of her flattered ego. This hand-on-mouth attempt at restraint was also employed to curtail the rapidly evolving possibility that her giggles could, at any moment now, explode into gusts of loud laughter. Moving rapidly along the sidewalk, she was able to catch a reflection of herself in a store front window. The glimpse of her reflected "double" caused her to realize she was repetitively doubling over, almost like a rabbi at the wailing wall, except her bowing was not in reverence but in long lost and now re-emerging humor and yes, laughter.

At the car, fumbling for her key fob, she realized "that guy" was not chasing her. So, why was she so hurried, giddy and shaken? "Well for starters," she reasoned, "that guy was actually coming on to me! Thank God, I apparently still have 'it', but I actually almost ran from that man. I mean, I don't think I am ready for a relationship, but how will I know when I am? Someday, maybe I'll know, and maybe this time I'll find someone as flexible and adventuresome like me!" Then after a pause, she added, "A fishing club has to be one of the most unexpected places I could ever imagine meeting a potential second husband." Then more soberly she supposed, "Should I be ashamed of that thought?"

About a week after her awkward departure from the bass club meeting, Hope remembered, also from the lecture, the name and location of a local fish store. With help from her car's on-board GPS, she navigated correctly to the front door of the store. When inside, she learned from the owner of "The Fish Stop" that it was called a tackle shop. (In her mind she thought, "Who comes up with these names anyway? 'Tackle shop' sounds more like a name for a football store! 'fish store' makes more sense.")

The owner was helpful and kind but was quite preoccupied with reading a newspaper spread atop the glass display case; the front face of the case paralleled the shop entrance. Cascading over the top of that case were cool breezes coming from a nearby ceiling-mounted oscillating fan. Its 1950's style gave a "down home/you came to the right place" feel to the shop. And the breezes helped stir the air, to some extent, in what would have otherwise been a musty smelling but well-stocked store. The owner sat not too far from the counter-top cash register as he gazed at the latest copy of "American Bass Angler". He was totally engrossed with its multi-colored multi-paged depictions of one bucket-mouthed bass after another. Most of them had been caught by a grinning, obviously corporate-sponsored angler. Not wanting to be too bothersome, she sheepishly interrupted him to inquire where she might find some rip baits. In response, the preoccupied owner looked up long enough to give her directions via a raised hand and pointing index finger. He had lifted his hand temporarily entrusting the task of holding down his newspaper to his oversized coffee mug. Apparently, coffee and fishing helped him combine two legal addictive stimulants; caffeine and the dream of catching "the big one."

As his head dropped back to focus on his "precious", Hope meandered in the direction the owner had casually pointed. She could hardly have known that Mr. Average was in her path, just around the first corner from the cash register. He had heard every word of her conversation with the owner.... the sum of which was not much. When she turned the corner, almost running into him, before either spoke a word, they shared one of those strange yet positive "synchro eyes" moments. Speechless, they stared at each other longer than was customary for disinterested strangers.

He was the first to finally speak. "Remember me? I saw you at the bass club meeting." She responded with, "Oh yes, I do remember you." Once they established that they <u>had</u> met before, he offered to help her with rip baits. She bashfully told him she didn't want to trouble him. He assured her it was no bother at all. In his heart he reasoned, "What could possibly be as important as time with you! Last time you nearly ran from me!" She gave in to his assurances, so they walked together to the store's impressive wall of rip baits.

As he explained various colors, "lips", weights and wobbles, he noticed she was sneaking occasional glimpses of him. She was thinking, "Mr. Average is actually quite above average in appearance. And he possesses such a comforting smile. More importantly, at this very moment, he is incredibly generous with his time. I'd better give this guy a second chance...and maybe a third." She thought about it for a moment than warned herself, "Hey, don't get ahead of yourself, girl!"

Their "chance" meeting pleasantly continued. Hope plied him with as many questions about lures as she could invent. His answers enabled his commendable patience to shine through, and his verbal kindness was obvious. He had considerable empathy for her hunger to know more about bass fishing. In an attempt to dissuade any potential embarrassment that she might have, he said, "Bass fishing is complicated so don't worry about any so-called foolish questions; there aren't any."

Well, you can only talk about rip baits for so long. So, now they were at one of those awkward pauses in the conversation. At this early stage of their introduction, further stretching this conversation to cover jerk and crank baits would have been an obvious strain. So, Mr. (now) "Not So Average" moved the conversation to a transition point. Not able to think of anything better to say, he offered to take her for a ride in his brand-new bass boat. She hesitated. He began describing its many features but quickly realized her eyes were sort of glassing over. He interpreted her nonverbal behavior to mean: "I am interested but I have no idea what any of what you just shared means." She was actually thinking, "I am not ready for more than friendship and does this man personally know my King?"

Before they parted ways, she asked if the former Mr. Average had a name. He teasingly reminded her he had offered it the first night, and it had been on his name tag. To herself she said, "That night I was so addled by your advance I couldn't have recalled my own name, much less yours!"

Correctly interpreting her semi-embarrassed "I have no idea" expression, he readily volunteered his name. "My name is Hunter." She thought, "What an ironic name for a guy who likes to fish." That thought was quickly followed by another: "Hunter! I like it!" He asked for her name; she eventually responded, "Oh, yeah, my name is Hope." He flashed that comforting smile once again. It was a special moment for both of them.

As if driven by some unseen, demanding schedule, they hesitatingly parted company with closing comments which included "until next time." Hunter was now encouraged by the fact that she had asked for his name. That <u>had</u> to be a good sign. But he realized she had not accepted or declined a ride in his bass boat. For now, he would have to be happy with the meager relational scraps she offered. Even though he didn't know much about her, he sensed she had been wounded in the past.

Hope was uncharacteristically cautious, not because she wanted to be, but because she was supposed to be. At least that was the protocol she thought would be held by most close family and friends and many not so close friends who might be critical.

Back at her big empty home she thought, "I sure hope that jerk and crank bait lecture happens soon. And Hunter had better be there!" She was already trying out their names together: "Hunter and Hope". Or should she reverse the order, "Hope and Hunter"? Either way, she liked the sound of it. Hope was finally starting to sense hope anew.

Their mutually hoped-for lecture finally rolled around, and with expectations exceeding that of just a good lecture, both were in attendance. They didn't sit together in order to avoid detection by any real or imaginary relationship spies. They did want the lecture to end, and soon. After all, there were bigger fish to fry this evening!

Finally, the lecture and the seemingly endless post lecture Q and A session ceased. As members and guests rose from their seats, Hunter made his way to Hope and again offered the token pastries and coffee. She accepted. He was encouraged by this, her first acceptance of something he offered. Well, nearly first, as he recalled all the info he had offered at the tackle shop.

Anyway, he was now thinking, "Should I attempt a second invitation? His self-talk counseled him to muster his courage: "The time is now dude; go for it!" It was hard to contain his nervousness. With his Styrofoam coffee cup providing "cover" half way between his pastry laden napkin and his lips, he re-invited her to a ride on his bass boat. (He needed a means to hide his anticipated disappointment if she rejected this, his second invitation.) But to his surprise, through a calm, "Yes", she accepted. Hunter clumsily replied, "You really want to go?" With tones indicating near reproof of his questioning response, she offered a drawn out, "Yeeesss!"

Having mutually overcome some degree of nervousness, they agreed on a date. But first, in the semi-private confines of a corner, she boldly yet graciously asked him if he was a follower of Jesus. She sensed he was, but definite knowledge of that commitment was crucial if she were to open her heart to anything more than mere acquaintance with him. When he said yes and backed his commitment with his story, she was relieved. After she shared how she had trusted Christ as her Savior, they returned to negotiating the details of their boat ride.

They agreed that Hunter would provide everything: the food, water, poles, reels, "tackle", ramp fees and of course tournament-ready brand-new bass boat. All Hope had to do was stand and wait at the curb, new fishing license in hand. The plan included picking her up at the end of her driveway. Being a morning person, Hope was pleased with the pre-agreed meeting time of 5:00 a.m. When she went to bed that night, she thought she would get plenty of sleep. But thinking about her first husband she just tossed and turned. She was wondering if it was all right to be so excited about her boat ride and maybe a potential second husband.

Her excitement interfered with multiple unsuccessful attempts at sleep. Her mind had moved on to actively recalling the details of their trip. "All I have to do is show up," she exulted. So "show up" she would! Lying in bed, she joyously decided to wear her best outdoors outfit and planned her "going fishing" make up.

As she thought about her ensemble, a bit of a mischievous smirk appeared on her lips. The smirk almost instantly began evolving into a full-blown smile caused by this thought: "Hunter, you are about to become the hunted!" Humbly, innocently she prayed, "Father, is it OK for me to think and feel this way?" Having heard no reproof from the Spirit, she sensed only inaudible peace of soul. As always, PaPa was right there with her.

She was just about to slip into some kind of sleep state, when the alarm clock on her nightstand, her cell phone and her tablet all rang at nearly the same time. All three had been set because there was no way she was going to miss her wake-up call. She rose from bed to execute her personal preparation formulated during her near-sleepless night. She was excited at the pure potential of this brand-new day. She dressed, put on her make-up, ate a quick breakfast then glanced at the clock. 5:00 a.m. had arrived; it was time to walk outside into the cool early morning semi-darkness.

As rehearsed Hope and Hunter met at the end of the drive-way. Together they enjoyed the brief, predawn trip to one of the largest lakes in their state. The sun was still about 40 minutes from fully emerging but everything was already starting to lighten up. Even in the early morning light, both marveled that there were so many shades of green this time of year. Hunter briefly stopped at the marina gate, but at this early hour there was no one there to show his annual ramp-pass to; he kept on rolling.

Their next full-stop was the designated staging area where Hunter went through his pre-launch routines. Hope wanted to do something to help in some way, but she realized at this point she would merely be in the way. So, following his instructions, when he came to the next stop close to the water's edge, she got out, walked out onto the dock, and from that perfect vantage point, watched him back up the boat trailer. When 2/3rds of the boat was in the water, Hunter shifted the truck to "park". Hunter accomplished all this like it was second nature. She admired his considerable skills.

From the trailer tongue of the boat, Hunter climbed onto the boat, then seated himself at the helm, where he quickly entered the boat's unlocking-code before starting its massive engine. She noted it seemed to be purring like a large cat. In order to slide the boat fully off the trailer and into the water, Hunter shifted the transmission into reverse and revved the engine. Now completely afloat, he quickly pivoted the boat 180 degrees, then deftly parked it right where Hope was waiting; it barely grazed the dock's bumpers. "Perfect placement," he thought to himself. He climbed out of the boat up onto the dock all the while smiling especially as he walked passed Hope. When he reached his waiting truck he got in then drove it and the trailer back up the ramp. Truck and trailer were parked in a single, long space. The space was one of many in the near empty lot. Noting the near empty lot, to himself he again thought, "Perfect! We might have the whole lake to ourselves today!" He then walked back down the ramp as fast as he could while maintaining his cool. Meanwhile, Hope's eagerness could not be contained. The tips of her powder-blue tennis shoes were edging closer and closer to the silver glittered, shiny gel-coated gunnel of the state-of-the-art craft. He proudly walked passed her then stepped right onto the front deck of his boat. As he turned to face her on the dock she was already asking, "Can I get in now?" He handed her a life jacket with his left hand while mimicking a seasoned sea-captain barking out, "Permission to come aboard granted!" With his strong right hand, he offered her a steadying grip. She appreciated his help...and touch.

Meandering through the marina they idled past dozens of houseboats and finally out past the "5 MPH" buoys. As they were about to take off, Hunter gave her a brief description of what was about to happen. She smiled, nodded and gave other nonverbal cues of her enjoyment. She wanted him to think she had understanding and experience of bass-boating even though in reality she had neither.

When they passed the last 5 MPH warning buoy, Hunter put the hammer down and the boat began accelerating. All three hundred horsepower of the high-performance racing engine cooperated, creating an impressive surge. The "hole shot" was precise and powerful. The bow of the boat rose 35 degrees off the water's surface almost like a jet about to go air-born off a Carrier deck. Hope's forward-looking view of the water was now totally obscured by the bow. Her eyes hungered for some angle that could reveal what was happening. As she scanned the shore on her side of the boat then the shore on Hunter's side of the boat, her happy eyes pulled back from far-vision to near-vision where they met Hunter's eyes. He had looked her way and his eyes were happy too. The acceleration of the engine created a roar and the resulting forward motion caused considerable wind noise, to the point they couldn't be heard without yelling. So, rather than yell at each other they simply reveled in the joy they saw in each other's eyes.

Initially Hunter didn't want to overdo the takeoff; he knew he could have really powered out from the 5 MPH zone. He chose not to do so in hopes of not frightening her on what he suspected was her first bass-boat ride. When he correctly read her happy mood, he decided to go even faster. At full throttle, with only the rear third of the hull in the water, now "on plane", they were gliding across the glassy lake at almost 80 miles an hour! Her shoulder-length blonde hair was now hopelessly tangled, but she confidently knew the rest of her designed-to-impress ensemble was intact. Actually, right now, she didn't care that much about her appearance. She was unashamedly experiencing joyous abandon. The beauty of the lake and speed of the boat resulted in thrills she hadn't experienced for quite some time. She was now laughing out loud. It was ok, because the tornado-like winds carried away any sound originating from her mouth. It was ok, because she saw that Hunter hadn't judged her for laughing. And it was ok to feel "such never done this before" euphoria. Then she thought to herself, "It is ok, right?" Although Hunter was laser focused on driving, by a quick peek he had witnessed her laughter. His engaging smile communicated approval and "go for it, girl" all at the same time. She was ok!

Nearing one of Hunter's favorite spots, they began to decelerate and come off plane. Hope wondered how long it would take for her heart to decelerate. She noted that being on plane was like an imaginary magic-carpet ride, only this ride was real. Relationally, she hoped they would never "come off plane".

They idled as close to shore as Hunter dared before deploying the boat's bow-mounted electric trolling motor. All was calm as they stealthily crept in to the targeted cove; its high canyon walls left it still mostly unlit by the sun. With both a cascading water fall above, and its gurgling stream slipping into the water's edge below, this was the perfect spot for rip baits. From the front of the boat, Hunter demonstrated the proper casting techniques; she admired his skills and abilities as well as his form. Hope then tried her first cast from the back of the boat. After several unsuccessful attempts, and with his encouragement, she finally got the hang of it. They tried the rip-baits for fifteen minutes to no avail. Hunter decided they would try something different. He deftly stepped to the port side of the boat's front deck then opened a huge hatch cover revealing a plethora of pre-rigged poles. He knew this was the right spot, they just had the wrong baits.

Now they were using rod and reel combos rigged with top-water baits. In a mere five seconds, it worked, big time! In a startling rush the fish "blew up" on Hunter's lure in their pre-dawn quest for food. Hunter was catching one bass after another and every time the unexpected "splash attack" of a large-mouth broke the silence, Hope would jump in surprise and laughter. Yet, to herself she wondered, "When are they going to take my bait?" Momentarily distracted by that thought as well as the shadowed beauty of the cove, she was forced to quickly refocus, when a two-pound spotted bass attacked her bait. Hoping she correctly remembered what to do, she started turning the reel's handle as fast as she could in hopes of catching what might be the big fish of the day. This her first bass was big, but not as big as Hunter's biggest. Comparing her catch to his, her latent competitive nature began to surface. Hoping to best his biggest catch, she wanted to get her lure right back in the water. But before she could make another cast, her latest catch had to be unhooked and released. Hunter showed her how to safely take the healthy-looking fish off the lure's treble hooks. To do so, he moved to her side; she enjoyed his unanticipated nearness. As he unhooked then tossed the bass, carefully, back into the lake, they looked at each other with shared joy and empathy; their affection belied the amount of time they had known each other.

As the morning progressed they fished on, moving to and from many of Hunter's favorite spots. When hunger set in, they joyfully ate their lunch in a quiet, tree-lined cove. After a few more hours of fishing, they reluctantly decided to call it a day. And what a day it had been and still was! It turned out to be one of those days people sometimes refer to as "yesterday" … as in "You should have been here yesterday!" They had lost track of their "catch and release" score at somewhere around 75 bass.

When they started their trip back to the marina, it was late afternoon. Hunter took the starboard driver's seat, and Hope sat opposite Hunter. He started the boat's eager engine then pointed it towards "home". With no hesitation at all, he advanced the throttle to the maximum RPM allowed but then he realized that would shorten their traveling time and consequently the time they would have together, so he eased off the gas pedal just a bit. As they glided atop the lake's surface, rocketing back to the marina, Hope was quiet-ly lost in care-free timelessness.

When they re-entered the 5 MPH zone, Hope scooted to the middle seat so she could retrieve a bottle of water from the hatch be-hind Hunter. She opened the lid, grabbed a cold bottle of water, then closed the hatch door having also closed the distance between them; she decided she wasn't moving back to her side of the cushy "tuck and roll" bench seat...no way. She took a refreshing sip and offered some to Hunter which he gladly accepted. The motor noise was still just loud enough to render impossible any real conversation. So, she sat there enjoying the twenty-minute ride through the marina. Sitting next to him she thought: "What other type of adventures does this intriguing man enjoy? Will he be willing to share them with me? And when it comes to trust in Papa, is Hunter willing to take faith-filled risks like I am? Could my adventuresome faith and trust in my King finally be matched by another? What draw backs might there be for two people who are willing to obediently 'go for it' as our King directs?"

Mid-thought, she succumbed to the need for rest. Last night's lack of sleep had caused her to dose off in a catnap. Then all of a sudden, she made the discovery that her head had slowly fallen on his shoulder which caused her to awaken with an embarrassing and considerable full-body spasm. She sheepishly looked up to meet his eyes and "yes!" his smile. He was not offended by her head on his shoulder nor her brief nap. However, he did find her full-bodied spasm somewhat humorous.

Though they were now near the dock once again, their hearts were still out on some imagined sea of possibilities. In their hearts, they were both now fairly certain this relationship had great potential. They would later find out they both had been pondering something like, "I wonder what kind of adventurous opportunities might lay ahead for a couple willing to risk all...for the King!?"

Couples Daily Devotionals: Faith Filled Risks and You

Day One: Start with a brief prayer, to help focus your attention on this time and to receive God's help. Ask the Holy Spirit to guide this special time.

1. <u>Bible Reading</u>: Hebrews Chapter 11:1-20.

    a. Take careful note of verse 6. Today, is pleasing God one of your highest priorities? Explain your answer.

    b. What are we to do when we displease Him? (cf. I John 1: 9)

2. <u>Journal Time</u>: Please record any "faith challenging" prayers. Remember to expectantly revisit the pages of your journal noting the prayers that have been answered and the ones that have yet to be answered.

3. <u>Prayer Time</u>: Ask the Holy Spirit to increase your faith so you can please Him more. (cf. Mark 9:24)

Day Two: Start with prayer. Ask God to help you set aside any distractions so your focus can be on this time with each other and God.

1. <u>Bible Reading</u>: Hebrews 11: 21-40 together. Having read the whole eleventh chapter now, which of the heroes do you

admire the most? Try to choose just one (each of you).
Share "why" you admire that hero.

2. Journal Time: Record some of your sharing; your prayer
    requests and answers to prayer.

3. Prayer Time: Pray for each other to have the same faith
    "practice" as the hero you choose; pray also for an
    opportunity to exercise that kind of faith today.

Day Three: Starting with prayer, include asking the Holy
Spirit to reveal something inspiring/encouraging to you during this
time.

1.   Bible Reading: Hebrews 3:1-11. Take careful notice of
     Hebrews 3:10 where we read: "And so I [God] was
     provoked (displeased and sorely grieved) with that
     generation, and said, 'They always err and are led astray
     in their hearts, and they have not perceived or recognized
     My ways and become progressively
     better and more experimentally and intimately acquainted
     with them'." Hebrews 3:10 (Amplified Bible, classic
     edition) Author's Note: the words "progressively better"
     and "more experimentally and intimately acquainted" are
     from the Amplified Bible, classic edition translation.
     There is lots here to consider which might make this
     devotional a longer exercise.

a. Of the following two choices, how would you rate your relationship with God? Progressively moving backward or forward? If you are not satisfied with your answer, consider ways you might want to pursue making your relationship with God and each other "progressively better".

b. Discuss some possible faith challenges the two of you might agree to "experiment" with.

c. On a 1-10 scale, how would you rate your level of "intimacy with God"? With each other?

2. Journal Time: Record any "action specific" answers from points a,b,c

3. Prayer Time: Ask God to give you the courage and resolve to act on your "action specific" answers to questions a,b,c

Day Four: Always start with prayer.

1. Bible Reading: Read Hebrews 10:19-25.

a. Take special note of verse 23. What are some specific ways the two of you can spur each other on to faith challenging "love and good deeds"? (Be specific keeping in mind how God "wired" your spouse.)

    b. What are some other synonyms for "spur on" that might be more motivating in light of your spouse's Motivational Value System® results or temperament?

2. <u>Journal Time</u>: Record any specific actions, dates, times that your "spurring on one another" will involve.

3. <u>Prayer Time</u>: Pray together asking God for wisdom and courage to follow through on your answers from about the love and deeds you are going to practice?

Day Five: Ask God to help you be encouragers of each's others faith.

1. <u>Bible Reading</u>: Read Mark 2: 1-12
Take note of verse 5. Whose faith was Jesus referring to? Do you have faithful friends like this? Are you one? Can you think of some ways to help you and your friends take some bold steps "experimenting" with their faith in God?

2. <u>Journal Time</u>: Note the day/date you request these kinds of friends for you and your loved ones. Come back to this page of your journal to record the date God answers this prayer for you and your loved ones. Include the names of people He brings in to your life.

3. <u>Prayer Time</u>: If don't have any "faith encouraging" friends, ask for them. Pray the same for your loved ones. Ask God how you can be one.

Chapter Twelve
One of These Days

Making Time for the Important Things

"Welding school?" The pounding beat and pulsing lights of the brief yet forceful commercial was making an impact on Manny. He wasn't sure what he would do with his life after his senior year of high school, but this infomercial was certainly giving him an idea. When the TV-voice-over fast-talked the instructions to "call this 800 number immediately," Manny was certain what his next step would be.

Everyone at Manny's high school was aware he was a great guy, the best in fact. Those who knew him longest knew he had been well-liked since elementary school. He was just one of those guys everyone liked to be around. Even so, and with graduation just months away, Manny still hadn't found the right woman with whom to spend the rest of his life. He knew the how-we-met stories of his extended family; most of whom had met their soulmate in high school. Not so with Manny. He loved people and enjoyed knowing many people, and being known by many people, but felt no pressure to find the right girl and settle down for the rest of his life. Often he would reason, "Why settle down when I am so unsettled? I have the rest of my life ahead of me. Why take on extra responsibility when I still have so much to experience and explore? There will be time for a wife and family, but that time is not now. One of these days I'll get around to being a husband and father and someday a grandfather; one of these days."

Manny sat in his living room, watching TV, contemplating more of his future. He knew that college wasn't for him; book learning wasn't his style or strength. But when he took the metal shop class his high school offered, the experience revealed he was exceptionally good with his hands. As his basic skills developed, so did his metal sculptures; they seemed to appear out of thin air whenever he was busy at his workbench. And my goodness, they were beautiful! It was obvious the man had emerging talent that just had to be recognized. Prompted by the shop teacher, Manny entered one of his creations in a competition held at their county fair. It was a simple but elegantly beautiful sign. He won first place! Encouraged by this accomplishment, he then entered his sign in a competition at the state fair. He again won first place and was offered considerable payment for his creation. But he declined the offer. He was going to keep it for the rest of his life as a memento of how it all started. It was already obvious: people wanted what Manny made.

What did the sign look like? Well, a picture is worth a thousand words, but this is a story, not a picture. So, I'll try to capture its beauty. Barely an eighth of an inch thick, it was simple, well-designed, durable, thought-provoking and artistic all at the same time. It was six inches high and sixteen inches long. The metal had been heated, immersed in oil then cooled in such a way as to reveal a deep palate of shimmering colors. Also, Manny had skillfully done some welding on the front side of the metal. A three-dimensional masterpiece resulted. There were only two words on the sign. They had been cut out of the raw material with a plasma torch. Welded on to the back of the sign was a royal-blue background. It made the cut-out letters "pop". Honestly, it is hard to explain how beautiful the sign was and still is. You just had to see it to fully appreciate it. And when you did see it, its message and medium would make you stop and ponder; which is what all artists hope for.

Well, high school graduation came and went. Competitions at the various fairs came and went. Manny usually won. But summer would soon be over, so the sign was wrapped and boxed. Protecting it was important. It was a treasure to Manny. He knew it would always be special and one day it would hang in his own shop, he hoped.

After graduation, Manny obviously no longer had access to the high school's metal shop. He was really missing the time spent there. And no welding shop would hire Manny without official training. Serendipitously, it was about this time the welding infomercial aired. Manny knew time waits for no man, so he decided to act.

Spurred on by his accolades and awards, but even more so by his ache to create, Manny moved to Southern California to attend the advertised welding school. Moving from his family's large two-story farm house in the Midwest to a studio apartment near his wielding school was not going to be easy. But that hardship was mitigated by how close his apartment would be to the beach. And when he anticipated homesickness, to comfort himself Manny would sometimes think, "Maybe I'll meet the girl of my dreams!" In fact, he did.

After loading the moving trailer, and saying good-bye to his family, the drive to LA was more emotional and longer than he expected. But still it was mostly pleasant; there were so many new things to see as he traveled cross-country. Manny drove his paid-for, mid-sized pickup truck, which was equipped with a towing package he himself had manufactured. Hooked up to his truck was his own mid-sized trailer (of course, Manny made that too) packed full with his bachelor-style furniture, basic kitchen equipment, clothing and a few personal effects. When he completed the last long day of driving, Manny finally arrived at the apartment complex he had seen on the internet. He went to the manager's office, got the key to his first-ever apartment then unloaded the trailer. Having parked the now empty trailer, Manny decided not to go back to his apartment to unpack boxes. Instead, he walked to the nearby beach. True, the boxes were waiting to be unpacked, but there would be time for that. He was hungry and curious at the same time; hungry for ice cream and curious about his new beach backyard. And that's when it happened.

The encounter with Carmen occurred at the base of the Huntington Beach pier. Both he and the woman that would prove, in time, to be his future wife were standing at the base of the pier eating ice cream as the sunset was coming together. It was a stunning scene: Sea birds were scrambling here and there along the water's edge hoping for one last sand crab meal before daylight was gone. Other birds, further back from the water's edge were sorting through picnic scraps left here and there by the day's beach goers. And out above the waves, calmly flying in "V" formations, squadron after squadron of pelicans were showing off their gliding skills. In what airplane pilots call "ground effect," the pelicans were able to glide inches above the blue, flawless, curling waves in "water effect." It was all so perfect, which caused Manny to wonder why there weren't any surfers. The waves looked so rideable and were backlit by pinkish cotton ball thunderheads outlined in gold. On top of all that natural beauty, the setting sun was shooting out rays 180 degrees. Its day's work done, it was about to take a dip in the Pacific for the night. There was hardly anyone else watching the sun go down on this day, an odd occurrence at the popular destination beach. But here they were, two young people at the right place and time, enjoying a breathtaking panorama that only God could paint. Starting with simple, polite "hellos" they advanced to casually chatting. They discovered they had much in common including not having had dinner before they separately had bought ice cream. With a winsome smile, Carmen said, "Want to get dinner?" "Why not?", Manny smiled back at Carmen. Carmen further queried, "Do you like Mexican food? I know a great sidewalk café that serves the best chili rellenos. They are to die for!" Manny wasn't real excited about buying store-bought Mexican food, but Carmen's excitement convinced him to try it. It turned out that he loved it; and maybe her? From that time on, whenever someone asked how they met, their story would always start with "Ice cream, sunset at the pier and chili rellenos." That was the day that Manny and Carmen started their lifelong relationship.

While eating their first dinner together, Manny found out that their apartments were within walking distance of each other, and that Carmen, a California native, was waitressing while taking some acting classes. She was good at roleplaying and memorization. She hoped to break into Hollywood one day. Carmen found out that Manny had just moved here from the Midwest (he wasn't even finished unpacking!) and had enrolled in welding school. But he made it clear his dream was to be a metal sculptor, not just an industrial welder. Both were inspired by each other's dreams. When the meal was over they agreed on a time and place to meet again which turned into a habit. It wasn't long before they took the next step in their relationship. At the base of the pier, Manny, ever the romantic, presented Carmen with a ring at sunset. They were soon to be Mr. and Mrs. Ramirez.

They were engaged just long enough to notify friends and family as well as develop a good plan for an on-the-beach wedding scheduled for December 3rd. What a holiday season it turned out to be! Their meeting, engagement, wedding, honeymoon, welding school and first home together all happened quickly and in a matter of weeks.

Now backing up a bit.... before their engagement, Manny had started welding school. A few weeks before their wedding day, he graduated at the top of his class making it easy for him to find a job. In fact, he had multiple offers. But his dream was to one day open his own shop where he would make a living "selling joy," as he liked to call it, the kind caused by his new twirling wind-blown sculptures. However, the realities of life including a shrinking savings account and unceasing "bills", made it obligatory for him to take a job as a welder at a farm implement sales-and-repair shop located north of Los Angeles in the San Joaquin Valley. The new job meant they were moving again, Manny's third move and Carmen's second move all in about 6 months.

Manny was excited about his new job; Carmen was fine with leaving hers. Acting would have to wait a while; she wasn't all that disappointed about leaving the Hollywood environment. For both of them, it was all happening so fast which made them even more determined to make time for each other, each day.

They moved and Manny started his new job. It had been easy for them to find temporary housing in their new town; so many choices. It was even easier for Manny to once again make new friends. One of whom was a customer whom most people called, "DJ." There were a lot of farming implements on DJ's farms which translated to a lot of ongoing wielding needs.

DJ Brown was a third-generation farmer with a massive amount of land under his care. When DJ found out Manny had just moved to the area and was hoping to find better, more permanent housing, he made Manny an offer he couldn't refuse. He offered Manny the small apartment on the second-floor of a huge out-building on his farm. This apartment hadn't been used in a while, so it was in need of some serious clean-up and repair work. It was offered to Carmen and Manny at well below market rates. Part of DJ's rationale was how convenient it would be to have a welder on-site and how much easier it would be for Carmen and Manny to save up enough money for a down payment for their own house. In addition to all that, DJ and his wife, Della, empty nesters, simply liked having people around. Combining the Browns, who liked people, with Carmen and Manny who were so likeable, resulted in a near perfect match. All the factors of this more permanent housing opportunity were so attractive to Manny but the piece that sealed the deal was this: on the bottom floor of this out-building was a welding shop. Perfect! Living quarters upstairs; welding quarters down-stairs. What could be better? With DJ's permission, and help, Manny added some gear to equip a rudimentary metal sculpting studio. After his day job, Manny would work there until bed time. To him it was worth it; he was doing it for his future family. And he knew that one of these days, hopefully soon, he would strike it "big" and become a well-known and well-paid artist. Carmen shared his dream.

Living in the San Joaquin Valley, married only a few months and still living in the upstairs apartment, one-day Carmen greeted Manny at the front door of their apartment with a pregnancy pee-stick in hand. With a big smile and hoping for one from Manny, she announced she was pregnant. His first reaction was shock. Manny didn't think their family would start this soon. In fact, it was quite the shock to them both when Carmen saw a "positive" result from the first pregnancy test she had ever used. Barely two years ago they were thousands of miles apart in separate parts of the U.S. contemplating things teenagers focus on like playoffs and home-coming. Now they were married and about to become parents. Yes, they were excited but a bit dazed too; this day had arrived so much sooner than either projected. Other than some morning sickness now and then, Carmen actually enjoyed being pregnant. It gave so much more incentive to "nesting" in their new apartment-on-the-farm.

Three weeks later, at their first doctor's visit, her pregnancy was confirmed. Manny was able to make this visit; he was glad to hear the baby's heart beat for the first time; it made it more real for both of them. The next prenatal checkup came at eight weeks. Manny couldn't make this appointment. After an ultra-sound, Carmen was given some startling news. "Twins!" She was stunned. She called Manny immediately to let him know and to get his much-needed emotional support. She really needed him, pronto! Manny informed his boss, left the welding shop, then drove to the doctor's office. He too was in a state of shock. After adjusting to the reality of twins, Manny and Carmen would eventually find out they had fraternal twins; a boy and a girl. Needless to say, their small upstairs above-the-shop apartment would soon be getting crowded. The day that they would need more room and maybe their first house came more quickly than their financial plan called for. But they were determined not to rush ahead and consequently miss these moments and, what years later would be recalled as "precious memories." When the twins were born, healthy and beautiful, the apartment was indeed cramped. "It's just temporary," was the encouragement they offered each other when they realized how crowded their quarters actually were. They resolved to make their apartment work while they looked for another home. Their search for something larger would find a quick solution once DJ heard what they were contemplating.

Out on a corner of one of DJ's other nearby fields was a house that had not been used in years. DJ explained to Manny, "Back in the day we used to lease and farm multiple sites; there were so many sites and crops that I needed a foreman. That house is where my foreman and his family would stay. We haven't tilled multiple sites in years, so I haven't needed a foreman. I tell you what, if you want to buy that house, a real fixer-upper, I'll make you another deal you can't refuse." DJ was right, Manny couldn't refuse such a once-in-a-lifetime opportunity. DJ was even willing to carry the note for the house which translated to the Ramirez's immediately having enough money for a modest down payment. Manny didn't want to carry the larger debt incurred by the smaller down payment, but he knew if he worked hard enough, one of these days, the debt would be paid in full and the house would be theirs.

Before they moved in, instead of paying a contractor, Manny did a lot of the needed repair work on the house. Remember? he was good with his hands. Of course, DJ was more than willing to pitch in and Della was willing to help with the twins and meals when they all worked together. One couldn't help but wonder if the Browns weren't trying to regain some of the time they lost with their own kids, now grown and moved away. Sadly, their own kids barely knew DJ. During their growing years, he was always working to provide a better life for them. Consequently, he missed so much of the life that was "now." These days, when the Browns and Ramirez's worked together, it was almost like a family affair.

Carmen and Manny moved to their new house a month before the babies arrived. It was relatively easy to move from the upstairs apartment to the foreman's house, less than a mile away. While Manny and sometimes DJ focused on the outside of the house, Carmen and sometimes Della focused on the inside. But with all the external repairs taking precedent before winter weather arrived, the inside repairs were behind schedule. They collectively reasoned it was better to make the house weather proof; inside improvements could be made along the way. Carmen hardly had enough time before the twins were born to unpack and feather her new nest. The essentials were in place, and she was fairly certain she could estab-lish routines that would allow her sufficient time to unpack and add the many Carmen-touches to their home. In time, it would no long-er be known as the old foreman's house, it would be known as the Ramirez's home.

In just a year, Manny's life had changed so much. He had so much to do now. He was a husband, father, welder, sculptor, entrepreneur, home improvement guy and he provided extra help on the farm as time allowed, of course. Then there were the ongoing needed repairs on the house (like the toilet leak that decided to occur in the middle of one rainy night) as well as the improvements that were needed in order to make this home "theirs." To have more time for Carmen and the kids, there was no time for TV, he had to quit his softball team (even though he enjoyed all the acquaintances it offered), and there was barely time for church once a week. Feeding times, diaper changes, meal preparation, dish-washing and laundry were all chores Manny chose to assist with as well as he could. No one could successfully accuse Manny of not having a good work ethic. Everyone still wanted to befriend Manny but with everything else on his plate, there was little time for developing deep relationships with anyone other than Carmen and the twins and Mr. and Mrs. Brown. All of his friends at the same age and stage of life agreed that when the kids grow up and move out, they would have more time for each other. When those discussions were held, and the Browns were within listening distance, if you looked closely, you could see the skepticism register on their faces; they knew better. From the school of hard knocks, they knew that the time to enjoy each other and good friends is now; they had paid costly "tuition" to learn that lesson.

The Ramirez home took shape, the twins grew. Manny excelled and advanced at work. More and better equipment was added to the welding shop on the farm. Manny's business took off. As the twins grew older they required less of Carmen's time, so she became the bookkeeper, marketing director, secretary and general all around "go-to" person at the shop. Della was more than willing to be a stand-in grandma. When they first opened the downstairs welding studio, Manny was selling a few sculptures to friends and at various craft fairs; business was especially good during the holidays. But as the beauty and quality of his work became better known, the demand for his wares increased. Every farmer in the valley wanted one of Manny's sculptures on top of their tallest building; his weather vanes were the best. They made great lighting rods, looked awesome (Their many moving parts made it easy to imagine staring at them for hours…like watching a well stocked 200-gallon salt-water aquarium), and they became something of a status symbol proclaiming to all "I am doing very well!" Manny and Carmen were livin' the dream; their dream. Their dream included having a big family. Which was about to be added to again. What a shock it was to discover they were about to double the number of children they had in less than two years. They were having twins again! The odds were one in 70,000 they would be so blessed. Manny and Carmen's parents were as surprised and excited as their kids. DJ and Della, the kids' on-site grandparents, were ecstatic! It was like they were getting a second chance to raise their own children.

With double the number of kids, a harsh realization hit Manny and Carmen. It was time for a bigger house. More bedrooms were needed. Searching for a nice house that was close to work, the shop and home wasn't easy. Frustration began to set in until at sunset one hot summer day, while drinking sweet tea on the front porch of DJ's massive but mostly empty five-bedroom farmhouse, DJ asked Manny if he had ever considered simply adding on to their existing house. Manny hadn't thought of it simply because he didn't have the money to do an add-on. Manny shared his thoughts about selling the house, knowing that the "sweat equity" he had added to the house would provide more than enough of a down payment to buy a bigger house. Manny went on to explain to DJ that another move to take a better paying job might be the answer, but together they reasoned that the meat and produce DJ generously offered from the farm more than made up for the increase in pay he might gain, not to mention the income generated from the sculptures coupled with the studio being rent-free. So, right there on the front porch, rocking chairs paused long enough to shake hands, the decision was made; Manny and DJ, now best of friends, like family, would add on to Manny and Carmen's house. Manny knew a good opportunity when he saw it.

Plans were drawn. Fees were paid. Construction began. Trenches were dug. Forms were poured. Framing was finished.

Once the we'd-better-have-contractors-do-this work was perfectly done, DJ and Manny, took over. They were already experts at working together and it was obvious; they had such a great time doing the plumbing, wiring, insulation, and even the drywall. In the added-on bathroom, together they tiled the new walk-in shower stall. This country-style beauty was now a three-bathroom, five-bedroom house!

At the end of one particularly long day, one continued long after their day jobs, Manny and DJ paused to admire the cabinets they had successfully installed. Almost like making a confession, DJ said, "I wish I had memories like this with my children. We could have done this together, but we didn't. I just didn't have or make the time. I was working so hard at work, then more work after that. It was too easy for me to justify missing soccer games, and day-time school plays, and picking the kids up after school. 'One of these days, soon' was my motto. But 'one of these days' became 'none of these days;' I lost so much. Don't you imitate me when it comes to your family, Manny." DJ's eyes were starting to tear up. Manny was wondering, "Is it okay for me to give this seasoned, grizzled farmer a bear hug?" DJ's need compelled Manny to do so. After a few healthy slaps on each other's backs, they broke their embrace, looked at each other, cleared their throats and without saying a word resolved to do a little more work before calling it a night. While DJ was still reminiscing out loud, sharing a few more woulda-coulda-shouldas, he came across a yet unpacked box. Manny and Carmen had started moving some of their boxed belongings into the newly created but not yet finished master bedroom. DJ noticed that the box appeared to have moved many times but apparently hadn't been opened in years. He asked for and received from Manny permission to open it. Inside the box was a package neatly encased in brown wrapping paper and tied with a cord. The package was a little over six inches high and sixteen inches long. It wasn't real heavy but heavy enough to cause DJ to be careful not to drop it on his toes. DJ couldn't help himself, he had to know what had such heft and required such careful yet substantial wrapping. Manny knew what was in the package. He hadn't wanted to open it just yet. But his love for DJ moved him to grant him permission to open the treasure. Quickly, yet careful not to let it slip out of his grip, DJ tore the string and paper off what was definitely a sign. DJ was awestruck by its beauty but not knowing Latin, he had no idea what its two words meant. In heartfelt reminiscence, Manny explained the history of the sign to DJ. He also pronounced and explained the two words he hadn't spoken since he crafted the sign in high school. With their meaning now clear, the two words struck home in DJ's heart. To Manny's instruction he replied, "With my own family, for me, 'tomorrow' never came." Tears that had been finished minutes ago began to flow again. DJ continued to share his quiet, reverential comments with Manny; but they were now short and to the point: "I wish I would have."

Non-verbally they somehow communicated (as only close friends can) that they were in agreement to not let a watershed moment like this pass; not this time. They stopped what they were doing, and with flashlights in hand, marched out to the old, dusty pickup truck; the one that had been on the farm for years. In near silence they drove the short distance to the welding shop. They left the truck, entered the building, then like two men on a mission, posted the sign in Manny's studio. What Manny had imagined in metal shop, only a few short years ago, had just become reality.

Above his work bench, as a reminder to both of them (and everyone else who would enter Manny's studio) were the two simple yet strong and beautiful words. Anyone who saw the sign was admonished to never, ever, assume tomorrow is guaranteed. In sync, through subtle tears, DJ and Manny, with mutually-felt resolution, as if making a pact, whispered the two words heralded by the sign: CARPE DIEM.

Couples Daily Devotionals: One of These Days

Day One:
1. <u>Bible Reading</u>: "Now listen, you who say, "Today or tomorrow we will go to this or that city, spend a year there, carry on business and make money." Why, you do not even know what will happen tomorrow. What is your life? You are a mist that appears for a little while and then vanishes. Instead, you ought to say, "If it is the Lord's will, we will live and do this or that." As it is, you boast in your arrogant schemes. All such boasting is evil. If anyone, then, knows the good they ought to do and doesn't do it, it is sin for them. James 4:13-17.

    a. Do you think the person depicted in this verse was acting on faith or presumption? What is the difference between faith and presumption?

    b. It is ok to have God honoring desires and to dream big? If you don't dream big, why not?

    c. What are some ways we can involve God in our "dream opportunities"? Compare you answer to Psalms 103:5

2. <u>Journal Time</u>: If you were to attempt your dream opportunity(s), what would it/they look like? Record your answer.

3. Prayer Time: Together, ask God to help you fulfill His "dreams" for your life. Do the same for your children, grandchildren, and/or nieces and nephews. And ask Him to show you the "next steps" needed to make those dream(s) come true.

Day Two:

1. Bible Reading: In Paul's letter to the Colossians he wrote, "Be wise in the way you act toward outsiders; make the most of every opportunity." Colossians 4:5.

    a. Who were the "outsiders" and what "opportunity(s)" do you think Paul was referring to?

    b. With your spouse and/or family in mind, what are some opportunities it might be wise to act on?

2. Journal Time: Record any of the opportunities the Holy Spirit brings to mind be they for your marriage, family, friends, etc.

3. Prayer Time: Pray for God to bring to mind some "outsiders" who He may be directing you to. Will it be to share the Gospel? To bring comfort or mercy or encouragement? Take some time to listen to what the Spirit may whisper to either or both of you.

Day Three:

1. <u>Bible Reading</u>: Psalms 90:12 says, "Teach us to number our days, that we may gain a heart of wisdom."

   a. What is the Psalmist stated goal for "numbering our days"?

   b. What is the implied reality if we <u>don't</u> "number our days"?

   c. Ultimately, where does true wisdom come from? Read I Corinthians 1:30 and Ephesians 1:17. How do you reconcile those two verses? (Hint: we already "have" wisdom through Christ but we need to employ it through the Spirit.)

   d. Which do you think "numbering our days" will result in fear or peace? Explain.

2. <u>Journal Time</u>: Record several circumstances or decisions that require considerable wisdom. On this date, note your concerns then check back regularly to see how God provides the wisdom needed. Together, include praise in your acknowledgement of God's answer.

3. <u>Prayer Time</u>: Help us to realize how short our lives really are. And nothing, save eternity in heaven, is guaranteed…especially not tomorrow.

Day Four:

1. <u>Bible Reading</u>: Revelation 3:7b-8a says, "…These are the words of him who is holy and true, who holds the key of David. What he opens no one can shut, and what he shuts no one can open. I know your deeds. See, I have placed before you an open door that no one can shut…"

   a. What "open door" opportunities God placed before you?

   b. What are some ways to discern between open doors of opportunity and those God has closed?

   c. What un-opened doors, if any, are available to you now? Will you "knock" on them?

2. <u>Journal Time</u>: Record your decisions to walk through those doors God has opened for you. Be specific.

3. <u>Prayer Time</u>: If there are doors you believe need to be opened, pray for God to do so. Pray also against whatever may be contributing to those doors being in a "closed" position.

Day Five:

1. <u>Bible Reading</u>: "Let us not become weary in doing good, for at the proper time we will reap a harvest if we do not give up. Therefore, as we have opportunity, let us do good to all people, especially to those who belong to the family of believers." Galatians 6:9-10.

   What opportunities to do "good" are available to you: everyday, seasonal, familial? Sometimes people have lots of good intentions but insufficient follow through. What is your track record for acting on these opportunities?

2. <u>Journal Time</u>: Record some of the opportunities you have to do "good". Include "when, where, how, who, and why" in a plan to follow through on those opportunities.

3. <u>Prayer Time</u>: Together, ask God for help in the planning and carrying out of these good works.

APPENDICES

Appendix A

How to become a follower of Christ.

It is up to you to choose whether or not you will become a follower of Jesus. However, be aware that you can't make yourself into his follower. Even if you could succeed by your own efforts to perfectly please God for the rest of your life, he would still reject you because of the things you have done wrong in the past, and for your part in a world system that has rejected God's standards. According to God's law, the wrongs we all have done are called sin (Romans 3:23). The penalty for sin is death (Romans 6:23).

But there is good news! God loves you (John 3:16)! So, he has provided a way in which you can be forgiven for what you have done wrong and made clean and acceptable to him. His Son Jesus, the one man who did nothing wrong and so did not deserve death, was put to death on a cross. By dying in our place, having paid the penalty for our wrong choices, he made it acceptable for God to forgive the sin of everyone who asks him to (Romans 5:8). The way is now open for us to turn away from doing wrong things then follow Jesus, who is now alive again.

So, if you want to become a true follower of Jesus, you need to take a few simple steps. You need to speak to God (Romans 10: 9-10). This is what is called prayer, but you don't need to do anything special like kneeling or putting your hands together. You don't need to go to a special holy place, but it might help to find somewhere quiet. Then you just talk to God. You might like to speak out loud, but God can still hear you if you prefer to do this silently. You can use the following prayer or adapt it as you prefer:

"Dear God, please have mercy on me, for I am a sinner.

I believe that Jesus Christ is the Son of the living God and that he died on the cross to pay my sin debt. I now know that through trust in Him, I can have forgiveness for my sins and a real purpose for my life.

I believe in my heart that death did not conquer Jesus, but that he rose again from the dead. Jesus' resurrection from the dead is proof that my sins were paid for and that there is obviously life after death.

So, please forgive me, Jesus, for every sin I have ever committed and/or done in my heart. Please come into my heart as my personal Lord and Savior today. I want to live for you on this earth and live with you in heaven forever.

I give you my life and ask you to take full control from this moment on. Please fill me with the power of your Holy Spirit so that I can faithfully follow Jesus as my master.

I ask this in the name of Jesus Christ." Amen.

If you prayed this prayer for the first time, here are some important things for you to know:

-It is important for you to tell your spouse and others who may have been influential in your decision. They'll want to celebrate this decision with you.

-Establish the habits of reading your Bible, praying and journaling. (These are explained in other appendices in this book.) You might start with reading the Gospel of John which the table of contents will show is the fourth book in the New Testament. If you don't have a Bible ask a Christian friend to help you acquire one.

-Become a part of a local church. Being with other Christians on a regular basis is very important. Just as it is very difficult for one log to burn on its own, it is difficult for one Christian to be "on fire" alone. Find a good Bible teaching church and regularly participate in person.

Appendix B

How to have a devotional time together

Why is it important to have a devotional time together? Simple answer? You want to develop every other aspect of your marriage: financial, physical, sexual, emotional, right? It makes sense to include "spiritual" on this important list. And in many ways, "spiritual" should be first as it seriously affects every other aspect of your marriage and family as well as all other relationships. You may be asking, "So how do we do this?" Great question! Here's some things to consider:

1. Agree on a time: Whatever the time may be, morning, noon or night, agree to do your best to stick to this time together with God. Agreeing on a time will help you avoid the "hit or miss" approach to this all-important meeting together with God. Agreeing on a meeting time includes agreeing on a time frame. Decide what is a reasonable time for the two of you to spend together with God. You might start with a shorter time frame, say ten to fifteen minutes. You can always expand this time as/if your schedule allows.

2. Agree on a location: This, along with your established time, will improve the potential for success. Typically, having a devotional time together once you are in bed won't work...especially if you are tired. Maybe meet at your dinner table or in your living room. Make this a special place for just the two of you. If that is not possible in your home, you might want to find an outside or nearby location you can depend on for being quiet and exclusive. Location is important but not super important; just a place you both know is "yours" for time with God and each other.

3. Stock your location: Be sure to have adequate lighting, writing materials, your Bible, reading glasses (if needed), blankets, a beverage etc. If possible, make the location a place you look forward to being at; warm and inviting.

4. Adopt a format: If you are doing couples' devotionals for the first time, this book includes a suggested format. It includes daily: Prayer, Bible readings, and Journaling (PBJ). You also might want to include spoken or musical worship. Adopting a format will assist in establishing the habit/pattern of a devotional time together. Having an agreed upon format will also help you avoid wasting time by having to repeatedly decide what to do. Once you establish the spiritual discipline of devotional time together, feel free to add/delete/adjust this meeting as needed.

5. Pray together: Praying, simply put, is communicating with God. Communication implies listening as well as talking. God wants to hear our requests, our cares, struggles, concerns etc. But he also wants us to hear Him; to listen. Sometimes He speaks to our hearts. Sometimes He uses other people to speak to us, like your spouse. Sometimes He uses the Bible (which is one of the reasons why it is important to have it available and to read it together). Sometimes to hear God's voice we need to slow down and meditate on what His Word (the Bible) says.

6. Journal together: Journaling simply refers to recording some of your thoughts, prayers, goals, ideas, plans and anything you sense God has placed on your hearts. It is a great way to help you stay focused on the topic(s) you are considering. It also becomes a wonderful record of God's provision; his power, supply, help, deliverance. It can provide a valuable legacy for your extended family.

7. Don't give up: It takes about 21 days to establish a new simple discipline. Longer time is needed to establish a more demanding discipline. So, go easy on yourself if you miss a few days or your time together doesn't go as well as you hope every time. Be patient with yourself and each other. How many times you stop having a devotional time together

is less important than how many times you re-start it. Be flexible. If your new plan isn't working, go back to step one and start again by establishing a new time, location etc.

Appendix C

Group Meetings

A couple once told me they have been meeting for the last 20 years with seven other couples for the purpose of encouraging each other to keep growing in and improving their marriages. That is a worthy pursuit!

"Short Stories for the Long Haul", in my experience, can be a great way to start a small group gathering. By the time your group, especially after attending a "SoulmatesForLife" training event, has worked its way through all 12 groups sessions of this book, the majority will likely want to keep on meeting. That's great! The format of the group meetings includes: Group sharing, prayer, Bible study, and "Strength Deployment Inventory* review questions."

The chapters are not laid out in any particular order. Feel free to use them in whatever order your group chooses. If your group meets for an hour, I don't think you will be able to cover all the material offered here. You know your group better than most, so feel free to "pick and choose" what you want to cover.

Chapter One
GOING DEEP: Class Overview

Purpose
The purpose of this lesson is to encourage couples to begin to share deeply about themselves with each other. It is hoped couples will work at creating a safe environment with each other in order to further enhance a growing awareness, appreciation and love for each other…and for the unique way God has created each person.

Overview of "Going Deep" Group Meeting
1. Feedback Time: How did it go this past week with the devotional PBJ's? 10-15 minutes
   a. The couple's PBJ includes: brief opening Prayer, Bible reading, Journal Time, Closing Prayer time (including requests).
   b. What did and didn't work?
2. Bible and Assessment Time: We will cover the "Going Deep" from both Biblical and Strength Deployment Inventory* (SDI®) assessment angles. 25-30 minutes. The main scripture passage for this week is Philippians 1:3-8.
3. Class prayer time: Pray for any requests; share answers/praises. 10-15 minutes
4. Reminder: Please do the daily devotionals and read the next short story at least 24 hours prior to the next class.
   Be flexible. You can cover these elements of your group session in any order that works for you and others.

Bible, Short Story and SDI® Time: 25-30 minutes

Bible Time: (overarching verse: "You husbands in the same way, live with your wives in an understanding way...") I Peter 3:7a (NASB)

1. Read Philippians 1:3-11.
   a. How does the world stereotypically identify someone who is in love? How is it the same/different from Paul's

depiction in Phil. 1:3-8? Can those who don't know Christ love like those who do? Explain.

b. Name some of the Apostle's strong emotions and love for his friends. How did these (emotions/love) come into being?

c. What actions arose out of Paul's love for his friends (vv. 9-11)? Which of those actions do you think Christians need to practice more? Why? What actions need to be more prevalent in your marriage?

2. In the Old Testament what does the word "know" mean? ("Know" has multiple meanings in the Hebrew language). Here are three different meanings:

- Yada: (pronounced "Yay-dah") means to deeply know (See: Gen. 4:1, Ps. 139:1; Jer. 1:5). This word describes the most intimate acquaintance – (Theological Wordbook of the Old Testament p. 366 Vol. 1). Yada can also have sexual connotations to it. In the context of marriage, it can mean "knowing" your spouse.

- Sod – (pronounced "sowed" with a long "o") means to be known by another person. In the marriage context it would mean being known by your spouse. It describes vulnerable disclosure. The primary meaning of the word includes confidential speech. It can also indicate a circle of intimate friends who give their advice (Prov. 15:22). Prov. 3:32 says, "For the Lord detests a perverse man, but takes the upright into his confidence." The word here translated "confidence" is the Hebrew word "sod"; it implies "secret counsel."

  Here's a great discussion question: "What do you need to do if we are going to be known by your spouse?"

- Sakan (pronounced "Saykhan") –describes "caring involvement." Sakan means "to be of use, service, or profit"; to be intimately acquainted and/or caringly involved." In Psalms 139:3 we read, "You discern my going out and my lying down; you are familiar (sakan) with all my ways." In the context of marriage, this would mean to be caringly involved in the needs of our spouse.

Summary: So, the type of intimacy we are striving for could be described this way: <u>Deep mutual knowing for the purpose of caring involvement</u>; oneness, not alone. (Cf. Intimate Life: Keith Ferguson) You might want to memorize the underlined words so you always have in mind what it means to truly "know" each other.

    a. Do you agree/disagree with the following statement? "God intends a husband and wife to know each other deeply." Explain your agreement or disagreement.

    b. If you agree that God intends a husband and wife to know each other deeply, what are some of the resources He has provided us with to know each other deeply?

    c. If you disagree that God intends a husband and wife to know each other deeply, why? What are some things that might keep a husband/wife from deeply knowing each other deeply? From deeply sharing with each other?

3. In the Garden, how did God provide for Adam and Eve's three basic human needs? (Acceptance, Security, Significance)

    a. Why did they reject His provision?

    b. What did Adam and Eve do in their attempt to hide from God? (See Genesis 3:18)

    c. What did their hiding accomplish?

    d. Why do we sometimes hide from each other? Compare/contrast your answer with I John 4:18.

4. In Luke 11: 39-40 Jesus says "…. did not the one who made the outside (of the cup) make the inside also?" Jesus was teaching that the Designer of the universe made the inner man as well as the outer man.

    a. What was Jesus referring to when He spoke of the inside of the cup? The outside?

    b. Does it make sense that the One who made the inside and outside of the cup knows what He designed? What does this tell you about Him? About you? About His love and acceptance of you?

5. Each one of us is an unrepeatable masterpiece of His handiwork. Ephesians 2:10 states, "We are His craftsmanship (poema – the Greek work from which we get our English word "poem"). Who are you inclined to see as more of a masterpiece, yourself or your spouse? What does your answer reveal?

Short Story/Strength Deployment Inventory (SDI®) review time:

1. From the short story: Do you identify more with Lori's family of origin or Tom's? Can you share some of your experiences with the class?
2. What are some of the pros and cons of Lori's family of origin? Tom's?
3. Name the three basic human needs. In your opinion, why are the three basic human needs so important to give and receive?
4. Often times our outlook on life and each other is greatly affected by our family of origin, lies we believe, and our wounds/pain. Which of those three factors has affected you in a harmful way? Beneficial way? Explain.
5. How many close friends do you think the average person has? How many do you have? Do you think it would be wise to have more? Fewer?
6. In your opinion, is there a link(s) between a person's MVS® (Motivational Value System®) results and the number of friends they have?
7. What would be some specific action steps you and your spouse can take in order to go even deeper in your friendship/relationship? (This question will also be covered in your Day One devotional this week.)

Prayer Time: 10-15 minutes

End of Meeting Announcements:

Chapter Two
HOW TO FIGHT FAIR

Purpose
The purpose of this lesson is to help couples develop a Biblically based and agreed upon format for resolving their conflicts.

Author's note: Because today's lesson and this week's topic is so common, the learning format will be a bit different. I am specifically referring to the seven steps of peace-making included in this lesson. I trust this will prove to be a very valuable session for you and all those in your class.

Here are some additional Key Verses to consider: Take the time to review them before this session. (They will also be used in the daily devotionals.) Hebrews 12:15; James 3:14-18; Proverbs 11:12, 12:18, 18:21; Matt. 5:21-22; I Cor. 13:5b; I Pet. 4:8. Another great resource is PeaceMakers which can be accessed at HisPeace.org.

Overview
1. Feedback Time: How'd it go this past week with the devotional "PBJ's"? What did and didn't work? 10-15 minutes
2. Bible and SDI® assessment Time: Main scripture passage is Ephesians 4: 25-32. Cover the topic from Biblical, Short Story and SDI® angles. 25-30 minutes.
3. Class prayer time: Pray for any requests; share "answers/praises". 10-15 minutes
4. Reminder: Please do the daily devotionals and read the next short story at least 24 hours prior to the next class.

Be flexible: you can cover these elements of the group session in any order that works for you and others. Be open to the Spirit's leading.

Welcome, opening prayer, feedback: 10-15 minutes
Feedback Time:
1. Have people share their success/failure with completing the "in between" class work.

2. How are the three elements of their daily devotional "PBJ" working? The three elements are: Brief opening Prayer, Bible reading, Journal Time, Closing Prayer time (including requests).

Bible, Short Story and SDI® Time: 25-30 minutes

Bible Time:
Some possible opening questions might include:
How do most people fight? How do you decide who won?
Who taught you how to fight?
What are some things most people fight over?
     Read James 4:1-3. What causes conflict?
     Are the three basic human needs (acceptance, security, significance) sinful? Spiritual? Neutral?

Read Ephesians 4: 25-32.
     While we review the following seven practical steps for fighting fair, keep in mind, your Strength Deployment Inventory* (especially your Conflict Sequence®), this week's short story and God's Word.
1) Prepare.
    a. Agree to a "start time".
    b. Prepare to state what you think the problem is: accurately, truthfully, concisely.
    c. Pray for each other while waiting/preparing to meet. Include prayers for: willingness to speak the truth in love; that you don't let the Enemy establish a "foothold" in your relationship; that you avoid expressing the problem solely through your "filters".
    d. Review the Conflict Sequence® of your spouse. Consider where your spouse "goes" in conflict. For example: If they are "blue", in stage-one conflict they will "accommodate" in order to preserve the relationship, so be sure to help them clearly state the problem rather than minimize it or gloss it over.... etc.

    Next: When you meet...
2) Resolve conflict sitting down. Don't stand so you can avoid implying a "flight, fight or avoidance" posture.

    a. Exclusively devote this time to each other; no interruptions, no phones or laptops. If you have others in your house, tell them something like, "Unless someone is bleeding or something is burning, don't bother us." This is a sacred time of resolving conflict together. Treat it accordingly.

    b. Pay attention to your spouses' verbal, para-verbal and nonverbal language. Be empathetic to any apparent increases in stress/conflict. If you sense the conflict is escalating, be proactive by identifying it, praying for each other and maybe taking a brief break if needed.

    c. Practice "mirrored" listening i.e. sit like they sit, arms/hands situated like theirs. This helps reflect the reality that you are sympathetic and truly listening.

Next, as you meet....

3. Speak the truth in love. (Eph. 4:25)

    a. Do your best to state the issue (offense) in "I" terms...as opposed to attacking the other person via "you" statements loaded with infinitives. Bad example: "<u>You</u> always/never/every time get this wrong. You're the problem." Good example: Here's what I think happened _____. And here's how it made me feel."

        i. Try not to put the other person on the defensive. That usually only escalates the conflict. Avoid "trigger" words specific to their assessment color.

        ii. From your Strength Deployment Inventory*, keep in mind the various communication styles of each Motivational Value System (MVS®). For instance: "Reds" may appear to be escalating when in reality they are merely engaging. "Greens" may appear to be aloof or distancing themselves; they can sometimes take longer to respond. "Blues" may use a lot of words etc.

    b. Some people think that not having conflict in the marriage indicates all is well. But that may not be the case. In fact, Marriage Coaches Curt and Rhonda Hamner have written: "Avoidance of conflict is the number one predictor of divorce." Curt and Rhonda have also stated "conflict avoidance" may be an indicator the other person is so beat down they don't want to try anymore.

Next, as you meet...
4. Listen to each other empathetically, not defensively; be open.
    "Walk a mile in their shoes." Be kind and compassionate;
    tenderhearted. That is what we are taught in Ephesians 4 which
    says: "Be kind and compassionate to one another, forgiving each
    other, just as in Christ God forgave you." Ephesians 4:32
    a. Remind yourself to be aware of your spouses' "filters" while
        you are listening to him/her.
                And, as you listen be asking for the Holy Spirit's help
        to realize if you are listening solely through your own filters.
    b. Check for understanding. When your spouse comes to a
        natural stopping point, paraphrase what you heard him/her
        say to be sure you are accurately understanding what was
        communicated.
    c. If/when asked for a response, respond to emotion with
        emotion and facts with facts. Avoid responding to emotion
        with facts or, to facts with emotion. This is HUGE. This
        principle is built, in part, on Jesus's statement: "weep with
        those who weep, mourn with those who mourn." (In SDI®
        terminology this would be "match 'color' with 'color'.")

    Next, when you reach a point of apology/reconciliation...
5. Include the following six "contractual" words: "I am sorry, will
    you forgive me?" Respond with the words, "I forgive you". This
    helps verbally assure each other the offense is "Off the record",
    so you don't keep a record of wrongs. (cf. I Corinthians 13:5:
    "love keeps no record of wrongs")

    a. Please note the following: 1 Peter 4:8 (NIV) says, "Above
        all, love each other deeply, because love covers over a
        multitude of sins." "Covering is different from 'covering
        up'. If something is bothering you and it won't go away, you
        might be "covering up" rather than "covering" the offense.
        As Ephesians 4:25 states: "What this adds up to, then, is this:
        no more lies, no more pretense. Tell your neighbor the truth.
        In Christ's body we're all connected to each other, after all.
        When you lie to others, you end up lying to yourself." Don't
        accommodate ("Oh, it's ok.") when the offense is genuine.
        "Blues" might especially find it difficult to be this "blunt".

b. Also, take note of the restitution example of Zacchaeus (Luke 19:8). When it is necessary and/or appropriate, restitution can be a strong demonstration of sincere repentance.

6. Strategize together. The Bible teaches us that our Enemy has schemes to defeat us (II Cor. 2:11; Eph. 6:11). Agree to some strategies to defeat him, with God's help of course.
   Agree on and implement a plan for minimizing offenses in the future. Example: "I am sorry I said _____ in response to your reminder to take out the trash. I will really try to never say or do that again. I know you have asked me again and again to take out the trash. Honestly, I don't know why I don't remember to do it. Please, let's try a different strategy for reminding me to take out the trash. Let's try writing your request on the wall above the trash can. With the Holy Spirit's help, I will try my best not to forget it."

   Finally,

7. Pray together. Then maybe do something fun to celebrate your victory.
   a. Prayer: Affirm your spouse's design…thanking God for how He made him/her. Conclude your prayer with the pronouncement of a blessing over him/her and a renunciation of any stronghold the Enemy may have tried to establish in your relationship.
   b. Celebrate: Take out the trash together…or it might even be more fun to go get ice cream together!

   Comment: God intends our marriages…all of our relationships to be a witness for Him. He doesn't want us to fake "all is well" or act as prosecuting attorneys against each other. He does intend for us to follow His example….to be Peacemakers.

   SDI® assessment Time (from the short story):
1. What MVS® do you think Frank/Penny are? (What clues caused you to make that determination?) How does one's MVS® come into play in couples' conflict?

2. Knowing that behaviors change in conflict, what Conflict
    Sequence® did Frank and Penny demonstrate? (What clues
    caused you to make that determination?)
3. Can you identify the Frank/Penny's conflict triggers?
4. As a friend, what advice would you give them to help them
    communicate and/or resolve conflict?
5. Identify some ways your awareness of your MVS® and
    Conflict Sequence® might improve your approach
    (behavior?) when in conflict with your spouse?
6. What is the difference between opposition and conflict? Can
    either or both be helpful?
7. What would be some specific action steps you and your
    spouse can take in order to better practice the Biblical
    principles of conflict resolution?

Prayer Time: 10-15 minutes
1. Are any couples currently in conflict? Be sure to encourage
    them to ask for God's help before they leave this class. If
    any volunteer they are in conflict, pray for them to have
    God's help. Pray for them to be humble and to resolve the
    conflict peaceably.
2. Be sure to receive any other requests and pray for them
    before you leave.

End of session announcements: Be sure and encourage
couples have their daily PBJ together (daily devotionals) and read
the next short story at least 24 hours before their next class.

Chapter Three
SPIRITUAL WARFARE

Purpose
The purpose of this session is to help couples realize they are involved in a very real spiritual battle with a very real, scheming Enemy who is more than willing to use any strategy to "kill, steal and destroy."

Overview: Remember the weekly follow up class consists of:
1. Feedback Time: How'd it go this past week with the devotional "PBJ's"? What did and didn't work? 10-15 minutes
2. Bible and Assessment Time: Main scripture passage for this class is Luke 4:1-13. Cover the topic from Biblical, Short Story and SDI® assessment angles. 25-30 minutes.
3. Prayer time: Pray for any requests; share "answers/praises". 10-15 minutes
4. Reminders to do the daily devotionals and read the next short story at least 24 hours prior to the next class.
   Remember to be flexible and open to the Spirit's leading. Feel free to cover the elements of the group sessions in any order that works for you or that "happens". Just be sure to stay in the time frames allotted so you DO cover all aspects of this session.

Welcome and Opening Prayer:
Take the time to pray together before you jump into this session. Praying together can demonstrate dependence on God. This expressed dependence can be a great example for every couple that is trying to deepen: a) their dependence on God (for their needs) and b) their relationship with God and each other.

Feedback Time: 10-15 minutes:
1. Have people share their success/failure with completing the in-between class work.
2. How are the three elements of their daily devotional "PBJ" working? The three elements are: Prayer, Bible reading, Journal Time, Prayer time (requests/answers).

Bible, Short Story and SDI® Time: 25-30 minutes

Bible Time:

Key Verses: Luke 4: 1-13. Supporting verses: Ephesians
6:11-12; II Corinthians 2:11; I Peter 5:8; Luke 22:31; Daniel 10:12-
14 (Some of these supporting verses will be used in the daily
devotionals.)

1. Read John 10:10. According to the words of Jesus, what is
   the Enemy's mission? Have you seen his work in your life?
   Marriage? Family? Share your answers.
2. Will someone read Luke 4: 1-13 out loud to the class? This
   will help us see the Biblical reality of spiritual warfare.
   a. Observe that even Jesus experienced spiritual warfare via
      Satan's tempting attacks.
   b. From Luke's account, what three basic human needs did
      Satan use to attack Jesus? Can you match those three
      basic human needs with each of Satan's three attacks?
   c. From today's culture/world, can you give some examples
      of how Satan tempts and/or attacks us via the three basic
      human needs?
3. In the author's 30+ years' experience in marriage counseling,
   he has found that most marriage counseling revolves around
   one or more of the following three basic topics: finances,
   communication, and romance (or lack thereof). Obviously
   "finances" was a big issue, understandably so, for Rich and
   Karen. In what area(s) does the Enemy most often attack
   you? Again, of the three basic human needs (acceptance,
   security, significance) which does the Enemy most often use
   to attack you personally? Your marriage? Why do you think
   this strategy is so effective on you? Your marriage?
4. Has the Enemy established a spiritual attack pattern in your
   marriage? For instance, a specific time of the day/night...is
   there a recurring topic or issue?
5. Please read Ephesians 6:12. Greek expert Joseph Thayer
   wrote the following about the Greek word translated
   "wrestle": "a contest between two in which each endeavors
   to throw the other, and which is decided when the victor is

able to press and hold down his prostrate antagonist, namely, hold him down with his hand upon his neck". And Greek expert Kenneth Wuest wrote: "When we consider that the loser in a Greek wrestling contest had his eyes gouged out…we can form some conception of the Ephesian Greek's reaction to Paul's illustration."

   a. What is your reaction to Pauls' Holy Spirit inspired writing and these two experts' insight on spiritual warfare?

   b. Do you/we take spiritual warfare in the form of Satan's personal attacks and attacks on your marriage as seriously as the Greek's took the consequences for the loser in wrestling match? Do you now understand how important (serious?) it is to know each other's MVS® and Conflict Sequence®; and "conflict triggers"?

6. What does "what-if-alley" look like to you? Why do you think you "go there"? What should we do the moment we recognize we are "going there"?

7. Consider the following two Greek words both translated "schemes" in the NIV Bible. In II Cor. 2:11 the Greek word "noaymata" can literally be translated as "designs". In Ephesians 6:11, the Greek word "methodeia" can literally be translated as "strategems".

   Commenting on Eph. 6:11, Wuest wrote the following description of the Greek word "methodeia": it describes…. cunning arts, deceit, craft, trickery; to follow up or investigate by method and settled plan, to follow craftily, frame devices, deceive; strategems.

   a. With these brief word studies in mind, what have you learned about the nature of the Enemy's attacks especially on God's people?

   b. How seriously then should we investigate and employ methods which can aid us in standing against him…methods like the "assessment"?

8. Starting today, aware of the various assessment results represented in your family, what are some strategies you can employ to successfully defeat the Enemy's attacks on you,

your marriage, your family? For instance: One strategy we are given is to resist the Enemy, quote scripture and worship. All of which are good, Biblical and effective. An additional, perhaps even more effective strategy would be to identify which of the three, basic human needs the enemy is attacking. Once that is determined, then one can resist the enemy not from a "symptoms" based resistance but from a "motivation/ three basic human needs"-based resistance. For example: Rich could resist the Enemy by quoting scripture like "greater is he who is in you than he who is in the world" which is true and good.

a. What if Rich were to fight back with scriptures that spoke of the child of God having "security" and "acceptance" before the Father via Jesus Christ? Example: If we are feeling hopeless:

   i. God's full acceptance of us comes through Jesus Christ (Romans 8). Therefore, in Christ we are secure for our entire existence; all of our days (cf Isaiah 46:4).

   ii. So, we can refuse to be hopeless via asking the "the God of hope" to fill us with joy and peace and to fill us with hope to the point that we "overflow" with hope (cf. Romans 15:13)

   iii. Further, if we are feeling hopeless about our needs, Genesis 22:14 tells us that God is our Provider. Since we are fully accepted by God through Christ, He is our eternal Father. It is His responsibility, as the Father, to provide for us. Therefore, we can be filled with hope totally secure in God's love, acceptance and provision "for and of" us.

9. What is a "test"? How is it different from a "temptation"? (I Cor. 10:13; James 1:13-14; Heb. 2:18,4:15)

SDI® assessment and short story Time

1. What would you say is Rich's Motivational Value System®? Karen's? What were your clues?

2. Can you identify the Rich/Karen's conflict triggers?

3. Which MVS® traits might be more inclined to correlate with strategic attacks by the Enemy? (Example: people pleasing, record keeping, preoccupation with being fair etc.) It makes sense that the Enemy would seek to corrupt what God designed for beauty and/or Kingdom purposes, right?

4. What unhealthy attitudes or behaviors did Rich/Karen demonstrate in their "before bed time" conversation? How might these attitudes/behaviors be linked to their MVS® behaviors? (This would be a good time to investigate the Strengths Portrait® and Overdone Strengths Portrait® assessments.)

5. OPTIONAL: Does Satan have a Motivational Value System®? If not, why not. If so, what do you think it might be?

Prayer Time: Take some time for prayer requests. Appoint someone to record the requests so people can give an update at the next session.

End of Session Announcements: Be sure and encourage couples to do the daily devotionals and read the next short story at least 24 hours before their next class.

Chapter Four
DEVOTIONAL TIMES FOR COUPLES: Group Meeting

Purpose
The purpose of this lesson is to increase your self-awareness and relational-awareness specifically applied to having a devotional time together.

Overview:

1. Feedback time: How did it go this past week with the devotional PBJ's? What did and didn't work? 10-15 minutes
2. Class teaching/discussion time: We will cover the topic from Biblical, Short Story and SDI® angles. 25-30 minutes. Main scripture passage is Isaiah 30:15.
3. Class prayer time: Pray for any requests; share answers/praises. 10-15 minutes
4. Remember to do the daily devotionals and read the next short story at least 24 hours prior to the next class.

Be flexible. You can cover these elements of your group session in any order that works for you and others.

Welcome and Opening Prayer:
Take the time to pray together before you jump into this session. Remember to ask God to help every couple deepen their relationship with Him and each other, depending on Him for a good result.

Feedback Time: 10-15 minutes:

1. Have people share their success or failure with completing the homework.
2. How are the three elements of their daily devotional PBJ's working? The three elements are: Prayer, Bible reading, Journal Time. Couples can practice these three items in any order they choose.

Bible, Short Story and SDI® Time: 25-30 minutes (label inconsistent with overview)

Bible Time:

1. Who, if anyone, taught you how to have a devotional time together? Can you share some of your experience?

2. Where in the Bible are we told to have a devotional time together?
   a. What then are the implications for married couples?
3. Read Joshua 1:8 and Psalms 1:1-3. What connection is there between "success" and meditating on God's Word? How might this be applied to couples?
   a. According to Luke 5:16, what is one of the ways Jesus practiced prayer? Since Jesus did this it makes sense we do too, right? And, the busier and more popular He became, the more He practiced getting away to pray. Is this our practice or is the inverse more accurate? Why? Jesus "withdrew" to spend time in prayer. Withdrawing was a very wise practical step to be sure he had time with God. List some additional practical steps that might really help couples have devotional time together.
4. Read Isaiah 30:15. "This is what the Sovereign LORD, the Holy One of Israel, says: 'In repentance and rest is your salvation, in quietness and trust is your strength, but you would have none of it'."
   a. Name some common issues that couples face today which require more strength. Name some common situations that need to be "salvaged".
   b. In this context, "salvation" can refer to salvaging a situation or problem. When you and your spouse are experiencing challenging situations/problems are you more or less inclined to repentance? More or less inclined to rest? What is the connection between repentance/rest and "salvation"?
   c. When you are in times of added demand on your mental/emotional/physical reserves, are you more or less inclined to practice "quietness and trust"? What connection is there with those two pursuits and "strength"? What disciplines does this verse suggest we practice to receive strength? What added benefit(s) might result from couples practicing these disciplines together?
5. Can you name some persons/powers that would want to keep couples from spending devotional time together? Why is it important to identify any persons/powers? Keep II Corinthians 2:11 in mind as you answer this question.

Short Story and SDI® time

1. In your opinion, which SDI® system best describes Roland? Valerie? Explain your answer.
2. From the short story: Do you identify more with the character of Valerie or Roland? Why?
3. What motivations do you think their (Ro and Val) behaviors are revealing?
4. What would be some effective strategies for lessening the conflict during their devotional times together? This week take time to note these strategies or "action steps" when you journal together.
5. In your opinion, what are their respective Conflict Sequences®?
    a. What might be the length of their Conflict Arrows*? Short? Medium? Long? Explain your answer.

Prayer Time: 10-15 minutes
1. Any specific needs you want to share with the rest of the group?
2. Close by asking God to give couples the personal discipline to set aside and use devotional time together.

End of class announcements:
Remember to do the daily devotionals and read the next short story at least 24 hours before their next class.

Chapter Five
ROMANCE: Group Meeting

Purpose
To help couples rekindle or further develop/advance the romance in their marriage.

Overview:
1. Feedback time: How did it go this past week with the devotional PBJ's? What did and didn't work? 10-15 minutes
2. Class teaching/discussion time: We will cover the topic from Biblical, Short Story and SDI® angles. 25-30 minutes. Main scripture passage is: Ephesians 5:21-33 and the Song of Solomon.
3. Class prayer time: Pray for any requests; share answers/praises. 10-15 minutes
4. Remember to do the daily devotionals and read the next short story at least 24 hours prior to the next class.
   Be flexible. You can cover these elements of your group session in any order that works for you and others.

Session Time
Welcome and Opening Prayer:
Take the time to pray together before you begin this session. Remember to ask God to help every couple deepen their relationship with Him and each other, depending on Him for a good result.

Feedback Time: 10-15 minutes:
1. Have people share their success or failure with completing the homework.
2. How are the three elements of their daily devotional PBJ's working? The three elements are: Prayer, Bible reading, Journal Time. Couples can practice these three items in any order they choose.

Bible, Short Story and SDI® Time: 25-30 minutes.

Bible Time:

1. What is romance? What is the world's view of romance? How is the world's view and the Christian's view of romance similar? Different?

2. Read Genesis 2:25. Why do you think some people are ashamed of sex? Is shame appropriate for a Christian couple? Where is the proverbial dividing line between shame and modesty? Is it best for a Christian couple to always be modest? Explain your answer.
3. Read Psalms 139:14. God designed us. How does that make you consider the issue of human sexuality? Do you view it as "necessary" or "wonderful"? What other words might you use to describe the purpose of sex?
4. Read Song of Solomon and 4:1-7 and 5:10-18. For modern day romance, what can we glean from these verses? What might be borrowing too much from these verses? Not enough?
5. Read Hebrews 13:4. What encouragement and warnings do we find in this verse? In the context of marriage, what does "pure" mean?
6. What are some ways to be romantic that don't involve sex?
7. Read Ephesians 1:6. This verse speaks to the truth that we are "beloved" of God.
    a. The Greek word for "beloved" is agapetos. Research/google what this word means.
    b. Consider the depths to which we are loved by comparing Ephesians 1:6 to John 17:23b.
    c. What does God's acceptance of you teach you about your acceptance of each other? How might your acceptance or rejection of each other affect "romance"?

Short Story and SDI® Time

1. What assessment results do you think Corinne displayed? What clued you in?
2. What assessment results do you think Terry displayed? What gave it away?
3. Which part(s) of Terry's plan did/did not address Corinne's assessment results? Whose assessment results was he trying to address?
4. Knowing Corinne's assessment results, what would be a better plan for the weekend? Be specific.
5. Can you think of things from their five senses list that Terry should have employed? What would your spouse prefer?

6. Right in the middle of the Bible is a not often read eight-chapter book entitled "Song of Solomon". It is an amazing love story. On the spiritual plane, it is a metaphor describing God's great love for His people. Yet, on the physical plane, it describes romance between a husband and wife. This week, read the whole book together, taking note of how all five senses are incorporated in their romancing. FYI: An excellent commentary on the Song of Solomon was written by Joseph Dillow. The title of his work is "Solomon on Sex". It can be purchased on line for as little as a dollar!)

7. What would be some specific action steps you and your spouse can take in order to better practice romance in your marriage?

Prayer Time: 10-15 minutes
Any specific needs you want to share with the rest of the group?

End of session announcements:
Remember to do the daily devotionals and read the next short story at least 24 hours before their next class.

Chapter Six
WHERE DID THAT COME FROM? Group Session

Purpose
To help couples develop greater self-awareness of what's inside their souls and how it affects their behavior.

Overview:

1. Feedback time: How did it go this past week with the devotional PBJ's? What did and didn't work? 10-15 minutes
2. Class teaching/discussion time: We will cover the topic from Biblical, Short Story and SDI® angles. 25-30 minutes. Main scripture passage is: Matthew 23: 25-28.
3. Class prayer time: Pray for any requests; share answers/praises. 10-15 minutes
4. Remember to do the daily devotionals and read the next short story at least 24 hours prior to the next class.

Be flexible. You can cover these elements of your group session in any order that works for you and others.

Welcome and Opening Prayer:
Take the time to pray together before you jump into this session. Remember to ask God to help every couple deepen their relationship with Him and each other, depending on Him for a good result.

Feedback Time: 5-10 minutes:

1. Have people share their success or failure with completing the homework.
2. How are the three elements of their daily devotional PBJ's working? The three elements are: Prayer, Bible reading, Journal Time. Couples can practice these three items in any order they choose.

Bible, Short Story and SDI® Time: 25-30 minutes.

Bible Time:

1. Read Matthew 23: 25-28. Which did Jesus assign more importance to, that which is on the outside (the behavior people see) or that which is on the inside (the motivation of one's soul)? In your opinion, do most church-goers practice

looking good on the outside or being pure on the inside? Explain your answers.

2. In Matthew 23, Jesus started His rebuke of the religious leaders with the words "Woe to you..." What do those words tells us about how important (serious?) is the unregenerate condition of one's soul?

3. In the short story, Lynn was astonished by the eruption that proceeded from her when she was in conflict. What are some possible soul-issues her eruption might have revealed? What might be some healthier ways to deal with those issues?

4. Read Romans 8:27; I Corinthians 1:20 and Revelation 2:23. How might the truth of these verses bring you concern? Comfort?

5. In Romans 7: 21-25, Paul shared the contest going on his soul. Can you specifically identify with his struggle? How?
   a. What assistance and/or assurance is offered to us in these verses?
   b. In your opinion, why do we put so much emphasis on external behavior (behavior modification) over internal behavior (soul transformation)? Give some examples of behavior modification and of soul transformation.

6. What are some reasons for hiding from each other what is really going on in our souls? Hint: Consider the three passions of the soul. Also, recall Adam and Eve's reaction to God's presence after they had "fallen". (see Genesis 3:10)

7. In conflict, how might anger be used to demand what you want from others?
   a. Is that acceptable? Explain your answer.
   b. Read Proverbs 29:11. According to this verse, what is the typical outcome of venting one's anger? Might this explain some outcomes in your marriage? How does the wisdom in Proverbs 29:11 differ from some modern-day advice?

8. Sometimes people excuse bad behavior with the words, "But that's just the way I am!" Is that truly an acceptable excuse? Explain.

9. Consider the following: Our motivation is "hard wired" but our behavior can change. Behavior might change based on culture, context, or becoming more spiritually mature. Example: Consider James 1:3 which states- "Consider it

pure joy, my brothers, whenever you face trials of many kinds, because you know that the testing of your faith develops perseverance." It stands to reason that our faith which can "develop" is growing and therefore "changing". So, everyone's heart can change, even in one's old age, right?

Short Story and SDI®Time

1. Proverbs 29:11 states that only a fool gives full vent to his anger. But doesn't one's tendency to prevail in conflict imply that some, by nature, will want to "conquer" and therefore should be given a "pass" on venting?

2. Many "assessments" measure "behaviors". The SDI® measures the motivation that drives behavior. What does your SDI® potentially reveal about the condition of your soul?

3. Behaviors often reflect what author Bruce Terpstra ("*Three Passions of the Soul*") has defined as issues derived from: lies we believe, family of origin, wounds and pain. What happens if we don't deal with these issues? How might they "erupt" out of our soul?

4. What connections might there be between obsessive/compulsive behaviors and the hurt, pain and/or sadness cooped up in one's soul?

   a. Can you name some common obsessive/compulsive behaviors?

   b. Once obsessive/compulsive behaviors are identified and the soul-connection realized, how might the Holy Spirit help resolve the issues? How might the family of Christ help resolve the issues? How might professional counseling help?

5. This week, remember to be sure to journal specific action steps you and your spouse can take in order to, on a daily basis, be more aware of what is going on inside your soul.

Prayer Time: This session has included some pretty serious topics. Pray for God's guidance and peace for each participant while also asking God to help them mature spiritually and in their marriage.

End of Session Announcements:

Chapter Seven
SPIRITUAL GIFTS AND YOU: Group Meeting

Purpose
To help individuals realize there might be a connection between their spiritual gifting and their assessment results. How might their assessment results compliment their spiritual gifting and that of their spouse and/or others?

Overview:
1. Feedback time: How did it go this past week with the devotional PBJ's? What did and didn't work? 10-15 minutes
2. Class teaching/discussion time: We will cover the topic from Biblical, Short Story and SDI® angles. 25-30 minutes. Main scripture passage is: I Corinthians 12:1-7, 11.
3. Class prayer time: Pray for any requests; share answers/praises. 10-15 minutes
4. Remember to do the daily devotionals and read the next short story at least 24 hours prior to the next class.
   Be flexible. You can cover these elements of your group session in any order that works for you and others.

Welcome and Opening Prayer:
Take the time to pray together before you jump into this session. Ask God to help each person to deepen their relationship with Him and their spouse, depending on Him for a good result.

Feedback Time: 10-15 minutes:
1. Have people share their success or failure with completing the homework.
2. How are the three elements of their daily devotional PBJ's working? The three elements are: Prayer, Bible reading, Journal Time. Couples can practice these three items in any order they choose.

Bible, Short Story and SDI® Time: 25-30 minutes.

Bible Time: – Main verses: I Corinthians 12:1-7, 11.

1. Have you ever taken a spiritual gift assessment? If so, what was the result?
   a.   What are some ways you can confirm the validity of your spiritual gifts test result?

2. In Ephesians 4:8, the apostle Paul quotes Psalms 68:18. In doing so he was telling us that part of Christ's prophetic mission was and is to "give gifts" to His people. He was referring to spiritual gifts. What does this tell you about the importance of acknowledging and using the spiritual gift(s) God has entrusted to you?

    a. How long has God known about the gifts He planned to entrust to you?

3. Paul wanted to be sure that the people in the church at Corinth were not "uninformed" (another translation says "ignorant") about their spiritual gifts. How can increased self-awareness through a better understanding of the "Three Passions of the Soul**" help a person become "more informed" about how God has designed them?

4. According to these verses, who determines "who gets what" spiritual gift?

    a. How might this understanding affect how you respond to people who feel you should have some particular gift?

5. What correlations can you see between how God has "hard wired" you and your spiritual gifting?

6. What are some of the differences between a spiritual gift and a natural talent?

7. In a healthy human body or by way of application a healthy church body (or team), all "parts" need to be present and functioning well. What correlation do you see between the "three passions of the soul" and having a healthy church body or team? Consider I Corinthians 12:21.

8. In a marriage, what are the advantages of both husband and wife having the same assessment results? What might be the disadvantages?

9. Sometimes we are tempted to think that our gifts are not needed or unnecessary. How would I Corinthians 12:22-31 address that kind of thinking?

10. In I Corinthians 3: 12-14 and 4:5 we read of standing before God to give an account of our lives. This is not referring to a determination of where one will spend eternity, namely "heaven or hell." That is decided on earth "in time." What is referred to in this judgment is the testing of one's "work" for God after one has trusted Christ as their Savior. How might

knowing about this judgment help a person understand the importance of knowing and using their spiritual gift?

11. Read I Corinthians 12:31 and 14:1. What does this tell you about desiring certain spiritual gifts?

a. Specifically, how does one go about asking God for a greater gift?

**"Three Passions of the Soul" refers to: Acceptance, Security, and Significance. These are the basic human needs all people must have in order to feel loved and valued. *Three Passions of the Soul* also refers to the book by Bruce Terpstra.

Short Story and SDI® Time

1. Of the three passions of the soul, which one do you think is Bob's primary motivation? Diane's? What were some of the clues?
2. What do you think was Bob's Conflict Sequence®?
3. Was Carl in conflict? How do you know?
4. How might you help a person in conflict get out of conflict?
5. What would be some specific action steps you and your spouse can take in order to better understand your Motivational Value System® and how it "links" with your spiritual gifting?

Prayer Time: 10-15 minutes

Any specific needs you want to share with the rest of the group?

End of class announcements:

Remember to read the short story, hold your group gathering, then practice the daily devotionals each week. Pretty soon it will become a good habit.

Chapter Eight
FOREVER HIS CHILD: Group Meeting

Purpose

The purpose of this session is to help individuals/couples consider whether as followers of Christ they think more like an orphan or an adopted child of the King. One might contemplate whether their soul is oriented more around an "orphan spirit" or "Spirit of Adoption". The self-awareness and relational-awareness that results can yield powerful insight about "why?" we do what we do. Have you truly accepted God's acceptance of you?

Overview:

1. Special preparation: Research the Roman Laws of adoption that were in force during the era the Apostle Paul lived. Share your findings with the class.
2. Feedback Time: How did it go this past week with the devotional PBJ's? 10-15 minutes
    a. The PBJ includes: brief opening Prayer, Bible reading, Journal Time, Closing Prayer time (including requests).
    b. What did and didn't work?
3. Bible, Short Story and SDI® time: We will cover "Adoption Spirit vs. Orphan Spirit": 25-30 minutes. The main scripture passage for this week is Romans 8:14-39
4. Class prayer time: Pray for any requests; share answers/praises. 10-15 minutes
5. Reminder: Please do the daily devotionals and read the next short story at least 24 hours prior to the next class.

Be flexible. You can cover these elements of your group session in any order that works for you and others.

Bible, Short Story and SDI® Time: 25-30 minutes

Bible Time:

1. Read Romans 8:14-17
    a. Paul was obviously writing this letter to the people of the church in Rome. As people who lived in Rome, they would likely be familiar with the Roman laws of adoption. Do you

know what those adoption laws were? (They can be readily found on the internet.)

   b. When you discover what those laws contained/implied, how might they impact your understanding of your "standing" before God?

2. In your opinion, do Christians consistently think more like orphans or adopted children of the King? Are there certain categories where some think more like orphans than adoptees? For example: money, answered prayer, healing etc.

3. Consider Matthew 4:3,6. What is the common phrase in both these verses?

   a. How did Satan tempt Jesus in these verses?

   b. Does this reveal a consistent "strategy" (cf. II Cor. 2:11) Satan uses in your life to get you to doubt your relationship to God?

4. When one is adopted into God's eternal family through Christ, it means one so adopted has become "royalty" (cf. I Peter 2:9).

   a. What title is generally given to the son or daughter of a king?

   b. How does this reflect on the way you consider/treat your spouse?

   c. What warning might this imply about spousal abuse?

5. Read Luke 11: 11-13. Take special notice of the titles Jesus gave the lead characters in this analogy.

   a. If you didn't have a good earthly father these verses are sometimes hard to relate to. What is the assumption about fathers in these verses? What is the comparison between "good" earthly fathers and God our Father?

   b. How might this "father/son" depiction affect how you offer your requests to God?

6. Sometimes we might think that God's provision is <u>entirely</u> (totally?) "conditional"; that "condition" being our perfection/performance.

   a. What might Isaiah 46:4 imply about the nature of God's provision?

   b. Do you think this is truer for certain MVSs®?

   c. How might this "performance mindset" contribute to an "orphan spirit" or mindset?

    d. Are there any conditions for being loved of God? For receiving His love?

7. Read John 10:10. What parallels do you see between the short story "Forever His Child" and the "abundant life" Christ has promised His children? Are you living in the abundance of Christ? Why or why not?

Short Story and SDI® time

1. From her family of origin, name some of the messages Li might have believed about herself/identity?

    a. What were some of the messages about yourself or "identity" given to you by your family of origin? Were they helpful or harmful? How might they be affecting you today?

    b. What messages from significant others in your life (teacher, coach, friends) have affected you positively and/or negatively? How might one defeat the unhelpful/hurtful messages?

2. Inside and outside the orphanage, how did people treat Li after her surgery?

    a. How did this treatment affect her self-awareness…her sense of being loved and valued?

    b. In what ways does our culture affect the way we view ourselves?

3. Remember Li's practice of smuggling buffet food to her room?

    a. What belief/thoughts did this reveal about the permanency of her adoption?

    b. What might be the analogous application for followers of Christ?

    a. What MVSs® might have a harder/easier time with believing they are fully accepted/adopted by God? Explain your answers. What help might those offer who have an easier time believing to those who have a harder time believing?

4. Name some positive ways Li perceived she was accepted? How might we use those similar ways today? How might God use those ways?

5. What would be some specific action steps you and your spouse can take in order to practice the mindset of an adopted child of God rather than the mindset of a slave?

Prayer Time: 10-15 minutes

Any specific needs you want to share with the rest of the group?

End of class announcements:

Remember to read the short story, hold your group gathering, then practice the daily devotionals each week. Pretty soon it will become a good habit.

Chapter Nine
IT'S A RECORD: Group Session

Purpose
The purpose of this session is to help couples realize that keeping a record of offenses is a natural human behavior, but they don't have to keep one. Couples can grow in their awareness of just how damaging it is to keep a record of offenses. Hate, not love, keeps a record of wrongs.

Overview:
1. Feedback time: How did it go this past week with the devotional PBJ's? What did and didn't work? 10-15 minutes
2. Class teaching/discussion time: We will cover the topic from Biblical, Short Story and SDI® angles. 25-30 minutes. Main scripture passage is: I Corinthians 13:5b.
3. Class prayer time: Pray for any requests; share answers/praises. 10-15 minutes
4. Remember to do the daily devotionals and read the next short story at least 24 hours prior to the next class.

Be flexible. You can cover these elements of your group session in any order that works for you and others.

Welcome and Opening Prayer:
Take the time to pray together before you jump into this session. Remember to ask God to help every couple deepen their relationship with Him and each other, depending on Him for a good result.

Feedback Time: 10-15 minutes:
1. Have people share their success or failure with completing the homework.
2. How are the three elements of their daily devotional PBJ 's working? The three elements are: Prayer, Bible reading, Journal Time. Couples can practice these three items in any order they choose.

Bible, Short Story and SDI® Time: 25-30 minutes.

Bible Time:

Key verses: I Corinthians 13:5b; Matthew 6:14-15, 18:21-22; Psalms 103:8-14.

1. I Corinthians 13: 5b says, "...love keeps no record of wrongs." How can one know they are keeping such a record? (Hint: Such a record can give evidence to its existence via phrases like: "Last time, every time, I have told you before, I have told you a million times etc.")
2. Can you agree to not keep a record of wrongs? If you DO currently have such a record, get rid of it. How? Write out your record, then go through the conflict resolution process given in the chapter on "How to Fight Fair". Attend to each issue, one by one, until all the offenses are removed from the record. You might want to involve professional help if this process doesn't go well the first few times.
3. In an old hymn written by pastor Charles Wesley one can find some fascinating lyrics. For instance, verse four of "O For a Thousand Tongues to Sing" includes the following words: "He breaks the power of cancelled sin, he sets the prisoner free."
    a. Do you agree there is such a thing as "cancelled sin" having "power"? How so?
    b. How can "cancelled sin" have power in one's personal life? In one's marriage?
    c. Who can break this "power"? What is our role in breaking this power?
4. Read Genesis 42:1-28 paying special attention to verses 21-22 and 28. How did past sins still haunt Joseph's brothers? Because they surmised Joseph was long lost or dead (verse 13), they must have thought there was nothing they could do to remedy their sin against Joseph. Ultimately, they would be given such an opportunity. But sometimes we don't get such an opportunity this side of heaven.
    a. What can be done to deal with a past record of wrong(s) where it is impossible or unwise to contact the person(s) who sinned against you or you sinned against?
    b. Is it always one's personal responsibility to make peace with another person? What if they don't want to be reconciled? Consider Romans 12:18 as you answer this question.

5. In this short story, do you think Whitney demonstrated a demanding spirit/attitude? What might this reveal about the yearnings of her soul?

6. Read Psalms 103:3a and 12.
   a. When we confess our sin, does God still keep a record of it?
   b. Is God capable of perfectly forgiving and forgetting our sins? Are we?
   c. If you forgive someone of their sin against you, but you remember it again and are tempted to bring it up again...what can/should you do? Consider II Corinthians 10:5 as you answer this question.

7. Read Luke 23:34.
   a. Jesus forgave those who were torturing them to death. How could He do that? What example does that leave us?
   b. When He forgave them, did they become "saved"? What needed to happen for them to actually become saved?
   c. What are some good strategies for being always ready to forgive? How might they help to not keep a record of wrongs?

8. Read Hebrews 12:15.
   a. Agree or disagree: The opposite of forgiveness might be "bitterness".
   b. What might be the "community/fellowship" impact of bitterness?
   c. How might bitterness contribute to keeping a record of wrongs?

9. Read Ephesians 4:26-27,31.
   a. Ultimately, who might be the source of an un-righteously angry and/or bitter spirit?
   b. Why would you leave him an opening in your marriage? In your home?

10. Read Matthew 5:9
    a. What benefit is there in being a peace maker?
    b. How are peace makers described in this verse?

Short Story and SDI® time

1. Which of the "Three Passions of the Soul"** do you think drives Whitney? Jason? What were the clues?

2. Can you identify Whitney's Conflict Sequence®? Jason's?
3. Which of the three passions of the soul might be more/less inclined to keeping a record of wrongs?
    a. How might that knowledge be used as an excuse or a "weapon"?
4. Is keeping a "record of wrongs" a gender-related issue or a Motivational Value System® issue? Explain your answer.

Prayer Time: 10-15 minutes
     Any specific needs you want to share with the rest of the group?

End of class announcements:
Remember to do the daily devotionals and read the next short story at least 24 hours before their next class.

Chapter Ten
OWNING WHO GOD MADE YOU TO BE: Group Meeting

Purpose
This lesson will focus on how uniquely and wonderfully God has made each human being. An additional emphasis is "owning" who God made you to be. Owning yourself and your SDI® results goes a long way in valuing each other. (Am I truly comfortable with being me? How does my strengths and weaknesses fit into the picture? Are my top strengths in line, or not, with my assessment results? Accepting the truth about yourself…so as to be "free" in Christ. Do I truly value my spouse?)

Overview: Remember the weekly follow up class consists of:
1. Feedback Time: How'd it go this past week with the devotional "PBJ's"? What did and didn't work? 10-15 minutes
2. Bible, Short Story and SDI® Time: Main scripture passage for this class is Psalms 139:13-16. Cover the short story and meeting topic from Biblical, Short Story and SDI® assessment angles. 25-30 minutes.
3. Prayer time: Pray for any requests; share "answers/praises". 10-15 minutes
4. Reminders to do the daily devotionals and read the next short story at least 24 hours prior to the next class.

Remember to be flexible and open to the Spirit's leading. Feel free to cover the elements of the group sessions in any order that works for you or that "happens". Just be sure to stay in the time frames allotted so you DO cover all aspects of this session.

Welcome and Opening Prayer

Take the time to pray together before you jump into this session. Praying together can demonstrate dependence on God. This expressed dependence can be a great example for every couple that is trying to deepen: a) their dependence on God (for their needs) and b) their relationship with God and each other. You might want to ask couples to get into groups of four then have them share with each other how the daily devotionals are or aren't working for them.

Call the group back together and have them share their findings and any tips they might have for using the devotionals.

Feedback Time: 10-15 minutes:

1. Have people share their success/failure with completing the in-between class work.
2. How are the three elements of their daily devotional "PBJ's" working? The three elements are: Prayer, Bible reading, Journal Time, Prayer time (requests/answers).

Bible, Short Story and SDI® time: 25-30 minutes

Bible Time:

1. Read Genesis 1:26-31. On the sixth day of creation, God made man and woman. What distinguished them from all other creatures God had made on the previous five days? What does this tell you? How might this affect your attitude towards your spouse?
2. The early church fathers (those who led the church in the first centuries after Christ's resurrection) recognized that we are "hard wired" to give and receive love. Are their "recognitions" in line with Biblical principles? Explain your answer in light of I John 4:7-8.
3. For centuries people have recognized that we experience love through the basic human needs/actions of acceptance, security and significance (Three Passions of the Soul). (Note: these basic needs are expressed via actions and attitudes. A helpful list of loving actions and attitudes is provided in I Corinthians 13: 1-13.) How effective are you at "loving" your spouse via acceptance, security and significance? If you have children, do they regularly experience your love via your expressions of acceptance, security and significance?
4. Read Luke 4:1-13. See if you can match each attack of Satan with each of the Three Passions of the Soul. What do you learn from this exercise?
5. Read Daniel Chapter 3. How were the three God fearing men able to be so "secure" in the midst of the threats of King Nebuchadnezzar?
6. Read Psalms 112: 6-8. What does this teach about the security God provides for His children? (See also Zechariah 10:12; II Peter 3:17)

a. In Hebrews 6:19a we read about God providing a firm and secure anchor for the soul. What is this anchor? Please share how during a difficult time in your life you have experienced God's provision of security.

b. How might the truth of Romans 8: 35-39 affect one's sense of security in Christ?

7. Read John 10:27-29. If we assume one has accepted Christ as one's Savior, then one is fully accepted by God as a result of having trusted Christ as one's Savior, right? And, since one is accepted by God, how might His acceptance affect one's craving for acceptance from others?

How might Paul's practice revealed in I Corinthians 4:3 help us not crave acceptance from others? How might I Corinthians 4: 3-5 and II Corinthians 10:12 help us when we are tempted to compare ourselves to others in order to bolster our sense of acceptance?

8. Read Ephesians 2:10. What insight does the truth of this passage give us about our God given significance?

9. How can the knowledge and practice of being fully secure, accepted and significant in Christ, free us to forgive and love others?

Short Story and SDI® time

1. What assessment results were portrayed by the main characters in this story? How did you make those determinations? Share the "clues" you picked up on.

2. Have the class do a wall exercise together. Put up four large pieces of paper on four different walls or locations. Have all the people of the same assessment result go to the paper with their assessment result listed at the top. Have them record two answers on the sheet: 1) What I like most about: reds, blues, greens. 2.) What I like least about reds, blues, greens. Have each group do this for the three colors not represented in their "at the wall" group.

3. When you typically think of your spouse, do you dwell on the qualities you like most or least? How might that affect ones' acceptance of one's spouse? Remember, "acceptance" is one of the basic human needs by which we perceive love. (Can you name the other two basic human needs?)

4. Give some examples of how owning your spouse's assessment results can practically demonstrate valuing him/her and vice versa.

5. What percentage of Americans do you think are truly comfortable with being themselves? Explain your answers. How does one become more comfortable with who God made them to be without condoning sinful attitudes or actions?

6. What might be some specific action steps you and your spouse can take in order to celebrate how God designed each of you?

Chapter Eleven
FAITH-FILLED RISKS AND YOU: Group Meeting

Purpose
The purpose of this class is to consider how one's soul design might affect one's willingness to take or not take faith filled risks.
Overview:
1. Feedback time: How did it go this past week with the devotional PBJ's? What did and didn't work? 10-15 minutes
2. Class teaching/discussion time: We will cover the topic from Biblical, Short Story and SDI® angles. 25-30 minutes. Main scripture passage is: Hebrews 11:6.
3. Class prayer time: Pray for any requests; share answers/praises. 10-15 minutes
4. Remember to do the daily devotionals and read the next short story at least 24 hours prior to the next class.
Be flexible. You can cover these elements of your group session in any order that works for you and others.

Welcome and Opening Prayer:

Take the time to pray together before you jump into this session. Remember to ask God to help every couple deepen their relationship with Him and each other, depending on Him for a good result. Leader, your goal for this class is to challenge couples to "experiment" with God; take some new faith filled risks in their walk with Him.

Feedback Time: 10-15 minutes:
1. Have people share their success or failure with completing the homework.
2. How are the three elements of their daily devotional PBJ's working? The three elements are: Prayer, Bible reading, Journal Time. Couples can practice these three items in any order they choose.

Bible, Short Story and SDI® Time: 25-30 minutes. Main verse Mark 10:27

Bible Time:

1. Have someone read out loud Mark 10:27. What was the context of this proclamation of Jesus? What IS impossible for God?
2. Please read Hebrews 3:1-11 prior to the class. Take careful notice of Hebrews 3:10 where we read: "And so I [God] was provoked (displeased and sorely grieved) with that generation, and said, 'They always err and are led astray in their hearts, and they have not perceived or recognized My ways and become progressively better and more experimentally and intimately acquainted with them'". Hebrews 3:10 (Amplified Bible, classic addition).

   Note and comment on the cause of God being "sorely grieved" with His people.

3. Have someone read Matthew 8:5-13. Why did the Roman Centurion receive Jesus' approval?
   a. If you desire to receive God's approval for your faith, can you name some ways your faith can be increased?
   b. What can you do if you just feel like you don't have much faith? One answer can be found in Mark 9:24.
4. Have someone read Hebrews 12:2. Who is the "author and finisher of our faith"? What does that truth mean to you?
5. What is the difference between faith and presumption?
6. Why do you think God uses trying/difficult times to stretch our faith?
7. Here is a good definition of trust: "Firm belief in the reliability, truth, ability, or strength of someone or something." Please Read Hebrews 11:1 then compare its definition of faith with the definition you just read. How are they the same/different? What do you learn from this?
8. Ask yourself, "Is my willingness to trust God evidenced by my/our obedience?" Please share some recent examples.
9. If you have time, do a quick review of the five devotionals for the week. Encourage your group members to stick with the couples' devotional plan.

Short Story and SDI® time

1. What, do you think, might be the MVS® of Hope's first husband? What do you think is Hope's MVS® is?

Hunter's? How did you make those determinations? Share the "clues" you picked up on.

2. Why do you think Hope was attracted to her first husband? How is that attraction the same or different with Hunter? Why do you think Hope's first husband was attracted to her?

3. What risks did Hope and Hunter take? What risks did either or both of them avoid? What typically keeps you from taking faith filled risks?

4. What might be some of the strengths and weaknesses of a couple with the same SDI® results? And in this case, two people who are willing to "risk all"? (Does any couple in this (your) group have the same assessment results? What can be learned from their experience?)

5. How might faith, trust and/or obedience be influenced by one's assessment outcome? Explain your answer.

6. As one becomes more spiritually mature, how might (might not?) that maturity affect one's behavior; one's MVS® over time?

7. How does my MVS® affect my trust and obedience and my (our?) willingness to take faith filled risks?

8. What would be some specific action steps you and your spouse can take in order to take some faith filled risks?

Prayer Time: 10 minutes

Any specific needs you want to share with the rest of the group?

End of class announcements: Remember to do the daily devotionals and read the next short story at least 24 hours before their next class.

Chapter Twelve
ONE OF THESE DAYS: Group Session

Purpose
The purpose this class is to help people realize how precious their lives and relationships are. Too often we waste time on things that are not important and the expense of things and people that are important. Sometimes we unwisely assume there will always be "tomorrow."

Overview:
1. Feedback time: How did it go this past week with the devotional PBJ's? What did and didn't work? 10-15 minutes
2. Class teaching/discussion time: We will cover the topic from Biblical, Short Story and SDI® angles. 25-30 minutes. Main scripture passage is: Ephesians 5:16.
3. Class prayer time: Pray for any requests; share answers/praises. 10-15 minutes
4. Remember to do the daily devotionals and read the next short story at least 24 hours prior to the next class.

Be flexible. You can cover these elements of your group session in any order that works for you and others.

Welcome and Opening Prayer:
Take the time to pray together before you jump into this session. Remember to ask God to help every couple deepen their relationship with Him and each other, depending on Him for a good result.

Feedback Time: 10-15 minutes:
1. Have people share their success or failure with completing the homework.
2. How are the three elements of their daily devotional PBJ's working? The three elements are: Prayer, Bible reading, Journal Time. Couples can practice these three items in any order they choose.

Bible, Short Story and SDI® assessment Time: 25-30 minutes.

Bible Time: – Main verse: "Be very careful, then, how you live—not as unwise but as wise, making the most of every opportunity, because the days are evil." Ephesians 5:16.

1. What warning is included in Ephesians 5:16? How might that warning govern what a person does or doesn't do in the course of any given day?
2. What does it mean to "be very careful" about the way you live? What is the difference between being "very careful" and being "very fearful"?
3. Does "making the most of every opportunity" guarantee "every opportunity" will result in a good outcome or success?
   a. Based on I Samuel 15: 22, which is more important to God, to obey (make the most of some opportunity) or to sacrifice (do something sacrificial but maybe not what God asked you to do)?
   b. We might think some "big" sacrifice is more important than some small obedience. How might God respond to that line of thinking? Consider Luke 19:17 as you answer.
4. Read Matthew 16:27. Is it worth it to do good? List some of the temporal and/or eternal benefits of making the most of every opportunity (i.e. "doing good").
5. What are some of the biggest time wasters in your life? What are some remedies for those time wasters i.e. what could you do instead that would benefit the Kingdom? If you need to repent from wasting time….do so.
6. Consider the promise of Joel 2:25. What comfort can this truth give to those who have wasted time on things that don't have eternal value?
7. How does one establish the balance between rest and sloth?
   a. How would one know if they are lazy? A workaholic?
   b. Is it ok to rest and relax; to withdraw from the demands of life?
8. It has been said that our lives are run by the "tyranny of the urgent" as opposed to the "important". How did Jesus respond to the ever-increasing demands on His life? Consider His example: "…the news about him spread all the more, so that crowds of people came to hear him and to be

healed of their sicknesses. But Jesus often withdrew to lonely places and prayed." Luke 5:15-16

9. In Galatians 5:16-17 we read: "So I say, walk by the Spirit, and you will not gratify the desires of the flesh. For the flesh desires what is contrary to the Spirit, and the Spirit what is contrary to the flesh. They are in conflict with each other, so that you are not to do whatever you want." How might "walking in the Spirit" help us make wise choices with all of life's daily demands in this post-modern world?

10. James 1:5 says: "If any of you lacks wisdom, you should ask God, who gives generously to all without finding fault, and it will be given to you." How can the truth of James 1:5 help us in making daily decisions about which door is open and which door is closed; or "good" versus "best" opportunities?

11. How might we know if we did in fact make a wise choice? Here's a hint. James 3:17 says, "...the wisdom that comes from heaven is first of all pure: then peace-loving, considerate, submissive, full of mercy and good fruit, impartial and sincere."

Short Story and SDI® time

1. In your opinion, what were the MVSs® of the main characters in this short story? What cues and clues moved you to your determination?

2. We all have regrets, right? In order to help him with his regrets, what wisdom might you offer to someone like DJ?

3. What might be some tactful ways to approach those who you feel are wasting their lives and or the relationship opportunities in their family? How might taking an educated guess about their Motivational Value System® help you in approaching them?

Prayer Time: 10-15 minutes
Any specific needs you want to share with the rest of the group?

End of class announcements:
Remember to do the daily devotionals and read the next short story at least 24 hours before their next class.

Appendix D

Outreach

It is strongly recommended that "SoulmatesForLife" training events followed by "Short Stories for the Long Haul" group meetings be used as an outreach tool. Improving one's marriage is something all married couples can relate to. The SDI® (Strength Deployment Inventory®) and SFL® (SoulmatesForLife®) materials are powerful and stand on their own in terms of usefulness and effectiveness. By the time most groups finish all 12 chapters of Short Stories for the Long Haul, they will have shared "life" in such a way as to have formed a life-time bond. It is the context of "relationships" that people often come to trust Christ as their Savior.

You can find a facilitator for Soulmates For Life at ConsentiaGroup.com. Another option is to get certified in the assessments and material provided by CensentiaGroup.com so you can become your own facilitator. Hundreds of pastors and leaders are certified and using this wonderful material in their ministries.

Here's a sample outreach letter:

Hey neighbor,

Well the holidays are over and life as usual begins again. Wouldn't it be great to start the New Year with a boost to your marriage? My wife and I would like to help. On Thursday night January 18th from 6:30pm to 7:45pm we would like to meet with you and some other couples to walk you through a time-tested assessment that is just now making its way from the business world* into marriage and family life. This is one of the best, if not the best training I have encountered. To say the least, I/we are excited about this.

My hope is to meet you, be a good neighbor, help you meet other neighbors…and for us all to expand our understanding of how to appreciate our spouses and each other. Here's some information that may prove helpful:

Dates:

Times:

Location:

Cost: There is no pressure to buy anything else or do anything else.

RSVP: Seating is limited to the first 20 people that register. Contact _____ at _____ for more information.

*For more information in hosting Soulmates for Life or for Certification as an instructor, go to ConsentiaGroup.com

ABOUT THE AUTHOR

Dr. Larry G. Shelton, a graduate of Azusa Pacific University, has post-graduate degrees in Medical Technology, Marriage /Family/Child Counseling as well as an earned Doctorate in Church Growth and Administration from Fuller Theological Seminary. Over a period of 33 years he led two churches, one of which grew from 70 to 3,000 in 15 years. He is married to the love of his life for 538 months and counting. They have five amazing children, all married, and five grandchildren. Dr. Shelton is the developer of the "Soul Mates for Life" application of SDI®. He and his wife, Faith (a surgical nurse) together find great joy in helping others advance the quality of their marriage and family. They reside in Northern California, enjoy the outdoors, and especially fishing.

Made in United States
North Haven, CT
26 April 2022

18603844R00134